Up The Lamb

This book is dedicated to the memory of my grandmother
Florence Edith McCarthy (1875-1951)

Up The Lamb
A Fictional Autobiography

John Ackerman

seren

seren is the book imprint of
Poetry Wales Press Ltd,
Wyndham Street, Bridgend,
CF31 1EF, Wales

ISBN: 1-85411-187-6

A CIP record for this title is available from
the British Library

*The publisher acknowledges the financial support
of the Arts Council of Wales*

Cover Images
Front: the author, his grandmother, aunt and mother —
his sister in her arms — Cwmdu Street, 1944.
The photograph was taken by the GI son of Florence McCarthy's
sister, who lived in America.
Back: the author as a schoolboy

Printed in Plantin by CPD Wales, Ebbw Vale

Contents

The true paradises are paradises we have lost — Proust

4

In My Granny's House

I was born in a red and yellow bricked terraced house near the bottom of a gently sloping street that led to the river, and still in the first awakening seconds I seem to hear the brook that ran alongside the house, at the foot of a high grassy railway bank, slightly widening as it joined the river. The river was a wide sluggish stream, crossed by a high stone-arched railway bridge, and was sometimes blocked with garbage, for everyone emptied the daily rubbish and ashes there. Often one or two dead cats bobbed on the slow-moving, stony waters. Later I was to paddle in these streams when trying to catch slimy minnows, and be scolded for falling into the murky shallows. Whatever the season, whatever friends one had quarrelled with or gangs one had left, there was always the river for endless fascination and distraction; its banks, partly fouled by ash-tips, offered all varieties of cast out rubbish, a much frowned upon but irresistible King Solomon's mine of refuse, and to the four-year-old gorgeous to behold. The stream runs swifter now, and more clearly, for the disposal of refuse is forbidden, and the children are healthier and no longer play there. But it is the legendary murky childhood stream that still whispers in the half-heard noises of sleep.

On the other side of the street, facing the houses, were the sheds, used variously as coal houses and lavatories; so that neighbours stopped for a chat on their way to or from the lavatory or while fetching buckets of coal, for the life of the street was personal, communal, spontaneous, hardly ever private. Beyond these sheds rose the steep grassy slope, on top of which ran the railway line. Time did not press urgently in this valley life, and we told the hours by the trains. There were only three important events: the early morning shift at the colliery, the afternoon shift and the night shift. Though there was, too, the school train which warned it was time to leave for morning school, and the early evening train, called the 'arsenal train' during the war when it brought back the men and women from the munitions factory in the nearby town: but these were lesser rhythms. The last and late train up the valley, patronised by revellers at the week-end, was called 'the rodney'.

This was the thirties, and the severe poverty of the depression in South Wales had not yet been ended by war. Yet while allowing for the sentimentalising processes of memory, one still remembers more laughter than hardships, the latter gladly forgotten.

Throughout these early years ran the presence of my grand-mother like a silver thread. I saw little of my father. He was a butcher, and the running of his market-stall was the centre of his life; and as my mother spent much of the day serving there, I was mostly left in the care of my grandmother.

She was a formidable woman, of strong will and of courageous character, with a sharp mind and tongue, and well read. She had wanted to be a teacher, and indeed, in the eighteen-eighties had stayed on at school in some temporary monitorial capacity. But she had left, her ambition unfulfilled, for the higher education of women at this time was costly and privileged, and afterwards as a young girl there were stories of her teaching the garden flowers. Florrie married Tom Ackerman, a tall, sturdy collier, less intelli-gent but equally zealous in his desire for the good life of working class idealism and Christian socialism. She taught him, as she later taught me before I was old enough to attend school, to read and write. Tom's particular passion was the chapel. Most of his short life, for he was killed at the battle of the Somme, was devoted to that place, which he had helped to build, being something of a craftsman. He came of a family famous locally for their physical strength, ability as rugby players, and a certain steadfastness of principle, though not for deep intelligence or social ease. 'You're bound to know the Ackermans! — Strong as a horse — and dull as two!' was a quip I heard generations later. There were also legendary tales of his brother who had survived the Somme and was a famous rugby player in Wales. But his magnificent play in the Welsh team selection game in Cardiff so excited the crowded arena that an admirer handed him an opened bottle of beer as he left the pitch, to intoxicating cheers. Alas, he took and drank from the proffered bottle. While the crowd roared their applause, it put paid to his selection. And there was no work in the pits, in spite of his skills, so he had to move to London in search of work in the post-war depression, eventually dying there.

Florrie, the daughter of a stonemason from West Wales, had married Tom in 1895 when she was twenty. At the pit Tom was much admired for his strength and fortitude, and his selfless devotion to his work-mates. He was always ready to risk life and limb for his butties when a roof-fall or explosion occurred. Miners were often trapped in the precarious, narrow gullies where they had to work and rescue was urgent and dangerous. Such was Tom's strength it was said he had an extra shoulder-bone, for he could use his arms and shoulders like a supple iron bar when removing fallen debris, heaving a fallen rock or boulder from the body pinned beneath. 'Leave it to Tom!' they confidently warned when a dangerous fall occurred; and generations later when a load of coal or other obstacle blocked the roadside 'Leave it to Tom!' was the local quip I heard, its inspirer long since forgotten. But Tom Ackerman could do nothing for his seventeen-year-old brother George who was killed at the pit bottom in Garth colliery, when the cage that transported the miners underground crashed down the pit shaft. It was Tom who identified and helped carry home his brother's body. Shared danger and comradeship underground forged the fine loyalty of miners, especially in the years before nationalisation when safety often took second place to profit. Ironically, too, it proved apt training for trench warfare in the First World War, when the generals were even more indifferent than mine-owners to loss of life. It was after a dispute at the pit, when Tom had crossed swords with the colliery manager, that he enlisted in anger, cheating his age — for he was in fact too old — and not telling Florrie till afterwards.

Wounded twice, Tom each time returned to the front, and once my grandmother visited him in hospital. But on his last leave he wept, even Tom, at the moment of departure, regretting too late having to leave his wife and five daughters, four of them young and still to be reared. He was killed soon after his return to the trenches. Seeking help from the parish poor relief, for her widow's war pension was meagre and could not be relied on to arrive on time, my grandmother was told by Major Thomas, the patriotic guardian of the poor relief, 'it's a poor hen can't scratch for her chicks!' In later years she forbade her daughters' attendance at the ceremony to unveil the town's new cenotaph, despite their tears at relinquishing the drama and prominence that was their name's bequest. Florrie's bitter epigraphs on war and victory gave scant regard for the patriotic pieties of stout generals and bland captains. Years and years later I was given the ribboned medals to play with, bright, unregarded tokens that gave more hurt than honour to Florrie, and were left in a jug in the dresser cupboard. The plate-size bronze medal, with Tom's name misspelt as Eckerman, long remained a dusty insult buried at the back of the dresser plates. In place of the lost medals I was given piles of the cartridges my father used when slaughtering cattle. They shone bright as brass, like toy soldiers.

Though keen in her chapel work and attendant interests, whether the Band of Hope, Christian Endeavour or Sunday School, in later years Florrie brought more passion to her political and literary enthusiasms. She read the radical literature and pamphleteering of the time, though she preferred the more dramatic and personalised literary forms, having a hard-won knowledge of Shakespeare, Milton, and the English novel in the eighteenth and nineteenth century — that is, the accepted 'classical' authors. Dramatic recitation was her forte, and she was much admired for her renderings of speeches from Shakespeare and the more vivid Victorian ballads at the chapel eisteddfods and, in later times, the pub concerts. My first acquaintance with literature was her declamation, with Welsh intensity and perhaps a Victorian inclination for the melodramatic, of such favourites as 'Curfew Shall Not Ring Tonight', which told of a maid who clung with bleeding hands to the clapper of a bell whose chimes should knell the execution of her imprisoned lover — dramatically reprieved at the last second; and 'The Wreck of the Mumbles Head', which I recall celebrated the valour of wives in the rescue of their shipwrecked husbands, and began, as my grandmother addressed her captive audience in Brechtian but un-ironic tones:

> Bring novelists your notebooks, bring dramatists your pen
> And I'll tell you a tale of heroes, of what women do for men.

Lady Macbeth's night-walking scene was another favourite, known to me by heart long before school, and seldom since has poetry so vitalised or drama so enthralled.

Tom had died of wounds in France despite his letters ending 'I hope you are as it leaves me, in the pink'. Florrie was left to raise five daughters on the war widow's pension, and as life darkened her radicalism fired and flamed. Of his sacrifice she would only comment bitterly that he was buried in the military cemetery, Bray. It was for her a symbol of the waste and necessary rejection of false patriotism — 'the old lie *dulce et decorum est pro patria mori*' was Owen's line she most often quoted.

Her energies flowered in Labour Party causes, for she was an able speaker and debater, effective on committees, arguing from principle as well as local detail, and a proud marcher in parades and demonstrations. She helped organise the local soup kitchen during the general strike, and in old age her proudest memories were of being on the platform when Aneurin Bevan spoke in a strike-scarred valley, and how in 1945 we watched, as I clutched her hand on the Downing Street pavement, an awed eleven-year-old, the State Opening of Parliament for Labour's post-war government.

Soon after the war, for she had her daughters to rear, in the direct, unsentimental, sturdy attitude the background demanded, she married Jack. Jack McCarthy, the grandfather I remember, was a vigorous Irishman from Cork. Of farming family, but a rebellious son, he had in un-Yeatsian style volunteered to fight for England. Jack's bravery on the battlefield in rescuing men from hit and burning tanks won him medals and promotion. But always afterwards he heard the sound of the guns in his ears, a haunting that remained. So surviving, he became a miner, meeting my grandmother soon afterward, and worked in Bryn pit, which he took me as a child to see. He never returned to, or indeed visited, or spoke of his Ireland.

Not long after the war the brightest of 'Florrie's girls', as my grandmother's daughters were referred to by her sisters, entered the local Grammar School, and my grandmother's passion for education seemed about to flourish through her daughter, who was totally devoted to her studies and would work late into the night in her bedroom, by the poor and secret light of the candle. But she seems to have been a frail, though charming girl, and when about to enter the recently opened Teacher Training College, where by chance I was to teach many years later, her remarkable school record and proudly won examination successes were no avail against the T.B. that she had contracted. She lay sick for many months, and there was no money to buy the costly medical care and treatment by which she might have survived. Reading to her day after day, in the front parlour of the inexorably dying, my grandmother watched the yearnings and struggle of that intelligent spirit with whom she so identified.

After her death the parlour was left an ignored part of the house, holding her books untouched for twenty-five years until, with my own entrance to the Grammar School, they became my inheritance. Entering that room as a child, with that total and unreasoned belief peculiar to childhood, I always thought that she was buried somewhere in its vicinity, so associated was she with it in family talk and so dominating the notebooks filled with that careful, loving copperplate handwriting I could never emulate. But I learned in Chemistry, Biology and Physics — subjects quite beyond my comprehension however much I swotted them — to copy successfully my own answers from those dry, meticulous papers whose musty smell I vividly recall. Of all the shocks that knowledge brings, and of all the divisions its cold light imparts, none was greater than the realisation, in later years of study, that that revered copperplate hand was not always infallible in its comments. Always keeping guard and watch there was the large family Bible, with its shiny metal clasps and colourful illustrations. In the centre of the plush-clothed table its pages were the repository of family documents, birth and marriage certificates, insurance papers, school certificates, and legal papers. It remained our archive as well as holy safe.

Florrie's other daughters, devoted and hard-working, like the eldest girl Polly who went out every day washing and cleaning to earn in cold backyards the few extra pennies towards her keep, seldom won her proud affection and high approval. Few communities held such unqualified respect for book-learning and intellectual discussion as this striving working-class world, where the Miners'

Institutes rang with the informed, passionate debates of the autodidacts, their minds precise and authoritative from their exact reading of Bible and political tract. Several friends, including Uncle Will, left the Tory pleasures of unemployment for the popular front in Spain, the war that aroused the strongest commitment. Returning wounded, Will Comrades spent his life selling 'The Worker' at street corners, though even he found work during the World War. But it was his singing of 'Comrades' that always ended pub evenings and my grandmother's parties, and singing it together was our true National Anthem.

Education and learning, rather than material success, were the holy grail. They forged the weapons, armoured heart and mind, in the dark and seemingly impossible struggle of working class communities against manifest exploitation and social injustice. The paths to fuller, freer lives were inexorably blocked, however green the valley. Not a revolutionary or violent people they instinctively elected education and the ballot box as the means of change, debate and withdrawal of labour their only weapons. Consequently those bright and hard-working enough to take the college path were devotedly encouraged, often through the unquestioned and unquestioning sacrifice of other members of the family. Undoubtedly, too, there could be an excess of zeal for academic attainment, as my grandmother demonstrated in her dismissive views of the different skills of her other daughters. One day Delia ran home excitedly from school to tell her mother she'd won the prize for housewifery, such were her skills at dressmaking and ironing. 'Trust you to get the prize for that!' was the dismissive reply from her stern, steely feminist mother. It was a wounding Delia never forgot. Ironically, in later years, such skills were valued — though underpaid — in the inevitable exile of domestic service in London, and both Polly and Delia joined the Depression's sad Welsh diaspora.

It was, I think, the tragic death of her favourite daughter that turned my grandmother away from her deeper concerns with education and politics. The enthusiasm at times recurred, but the ruling passion was allowed, perhaps encouraged, to die. As is so often the case, her religious convictions and devotions also became numbed. It was in people, company, and convivial rather than solitary, intellectual pleasures that my grandmother now found escape. She began drinking, and formed what became her own peculiar 'salon' at the local pub. This is the woman whom in actual, rather than imaginative, memory I knew, loved and grew to understand. The political beliefs and enthusiasms remained, and flared throughout the contentious twenties and thirties, but ultimate grief and irreparable loss had brought that deeper vision that does not see them as final panaceas.

So my actual memory is a friendlier one, touched more with comedy and joy than bitterness or eloquent crusade, though Florrie's tongue never lost its caustic and Victorian sententiousness in reprimand. One day her exuberant daughter Delia, who used to spend many hours making faces in the mirror, rushed to her in distress saying she'd seen the devil in the glass. 'You won't see anybody worse than yourself!' was her retort to this Alice-like narcissism. Nevertheless, though Florrie herself never sang, throughout their lives her four surviving daughters sang as they went about their household tasks, whether they were dusting, washing, or simply taking a rest as they gazed across the field from the pantry window. Similarly in later years, visiting or home on holidays, mothers and grandmothers themselves, singing was as natural to them as talk. They sang Victorian ballads, First and Second World War tunes, Welsh and Irish folk songs, and their voices were the babble of childhood streams that ring still in the silence of other rooms, later lives. 'I'll walk beside you', 'Keep the Home Fires Burning', 'Comrades', 'Ar Lan y Môr' and 'Danny Boy' then and always the silent and loud voices of exile.

Jack McCarthy, a strong, tough, gentle Irishman, always worked on the afternoon shift, leaving the house for the colliery at one o'clock and returning at eleven each night. Before leaving he would take me 'down the river' for the walk that was only a few yards, as the sluggish stream flowed at the bottom of the street, but seemed to me a journey of endless delight. In the day we would usually stop at the narrow wooden bridge that led across the river to the allotments, and he would tootle down there, in that squat position peculiar to miners that they seem to find so comfortable, to be joined by friends on their way to or from the allotments, while I roved among the debris on the river bank discovering the odds and ends cast off by the street. Sometimes we would join one of his friends and cross the bridge to inspect the neat plots of vegetable gardens, mostly started during the slumps and depression, returning with some apples or lettuce or blackcurrants, according to the season. A special thrill was to visit one of the greenhouses, and be given a few grapes, to return with a Mediterranean glow of triumph. Our placid dog Molly, who had a glass eye, accompanied, loyal but stumbling in her extreme old age.

Then in the early afternoon my grandfather would collect his tin box that contained bread and cheese, his jack of water, and set out for work. And always, whatever quarrel or tension there might have been, he would kiss his wife goodbye, and pat me on the head, because, working in the colliery, you never knew. And I had the whole long afternoon in which to play, or learn to read and write, tasks my grandmother's patient tuition greatly assisted. And even while at school I insisted, for the first months, in writing my full address as: John Ackerman, 26 Cwmdu Street, Maesteg, in my granny's house. I soon joined the nearby Miners' Library. It was in later years that North's Library and Institute was erected as memorial to the mine owner of that name, Colonel North of North's Navigation collieries. Many years later still and by chance I taught at a country-house style college, indeed a stylish house and gardens, that I was to learn belonged to Colonel North. I learned, too, that much of his money came not only from South Wales but also South American mines. The entry to his lavish mansion, within spacious grounds, was marked 1895.

The first excitement of evening, as the cat snoozed on the mat before the coal fire, would be when my grandmother sat in her armchair, and put her steel curling tongs between the bars. It was the sign she was getting ready to go 'up "The Lamb"', the local pub. 'The Lamb' was at the top of the street. As the tongs reddened she would draw them from the fire, spit on them, and wipe them with a piece of newspaper. Slowly she would begin to curl the wispy strands of grey hair, so that they gradually acquired a brown tinge. I would fetch her brooch from the dresser, her fox fur from the parlour, and her black coat from its peg in the passage, while the cat miaowed and grumbled, disturbed in his sleep by my excited, predatory footsteps, until he finally retreated under the chair, Molly making way for him.

'Can I come up, Gran?'

'Ask your mother.'

'He can go, if he wants to.' Then to me. 'Only change your trousers — you made that one filthy fetching the small coal. And don't pester me now, I've got too much to do! I'm all behind like a cow's tail.'

'Remember you'll have to go in the back kitchen if it gets too crowded, and under the table if the police come in,' said my grandmother.

At eight o'clock we began our short walk up the street, arm in arm since my grandmother's eyesight was failing and I was acting as guide. In the war-time blackout I carried a candle lantern, my dici-show-light in the childwood dark. Half way up, we called for Aunty Martha. We entered the house by the back door, where a quiet whisky awaited my grandmother, and Martha was always ready. But soon we were in 'The Lamb', seated in the corner near the fireplace, and the evening's gossip and drinking started. It was really a club, for each evening the same friends would assemble, and as part of my learning to write, I carried a register and would list the names of 'the kitchen friends', for they always sat in the so-named back room of the pub, as they arrived.

The pub closed at ten, but my grandmother and her friends usually drank until ten-thirty, then we had to hurry home, since 'Gugga'— so named by me — returned from the colliery at eleven, and my grandmother felt it behoved her to have some visible signs of the approaching supper on the table. Otherwise 'It's as bare as a rook's arse here!' Gugga would humorously complain, to my delight. Usually we only just made it, and my grandfather would arrive as my grandmother hurriedly laid the table cloth and put the potatoes on to boil, pushing some sticks into the fire so that extra leaping flames and crackling wood added to the sense of excitement. This was the main meal of the day, our appetites given an edge by beer and the savoury smells of the meat as it roasted in the oven. The cat sniffed the air and miaowed in anticipatory pleasure.

While the supper was being prepared, Gugga bathed in the tin bath before the fire quickly and without fuss. No one particularly noticed, it was as much a domestic routine as taking meals, and only the more slovenly miners and households took their meals before bathing. Usually my mother put the bucket of water on the fire well before his and our return, so that it could be placed, bubbling and boiling, on the hob until he came, and the red coals were ready for the cooking pans. This was the house's busiest time of the day, and I helped and hindered, getting in and out of the way. While my grandfather bathed before the fire, dexterously cupping his private parts in one hand while he soaped himself with the other, I assisted by washing his back. Afterwards he would sit at the kitchen table with the flagon of beer that my grandmother had brought, while I drank from the tin jack the remaining stale, flat water that he had carefully left for me, the most delicious, and jealously savoured water of childhood. To my grandmother he would say 'And how was Hell's kitchen tonight? Was Polly there?' And in turn, he would inquire which, if not all, of her daughters and friends had attended her soirée.

After supper, my grandmother sat in the armchair before the fire with her book, and would read till three or four in the morning. Even in sleep I would hear her slowly tread up the stairs, halting at the sharp turn near the top, then proceed along the landing past the gaunt Victorian family portraits. Her favoured authors included Jane Austen, George Eliot, Dickens and Thackeray, tastes I was never to acquire, as well as the detective stories of Sayers and Christie and Conan Doyle. When there was a Shakespeare play on the wireless she followed it in her 1897 edition of the complete works in a very small print. It was a bulky foolscap size volume that I sometimes helped to hold. I was impressed that it was published in the Tudor Printing Works in Cardiff.

At midnight, Gugga and I would set off on our walk down to the river, for I had to go to bed at twelve thirty, and it was our night-cap, prevented only by heavy rain. In darkness we could hear the splashing, gurgling river, but see it only momentarily in sudden moonlight. We nightly walked as far as the bridge, then returned from the river I always hear in the darkness before sleep and in the darkness of strange places however distant.

Up The Market

My father was a butcher, a ruthless, crooked, remote, confident, energetic, and violent man. Victim of his attacks on my mother, I was born in the eighth month — a baby purple in colour and two pounds in weight. The kindly doctor said I couldn't live long and tactfully added I could be buried in a box in the back garden, no papers or funeral needed. But luckily Aunty Polly, local seer and fortune teller, said I should be fed brandy, not milk. And the bottle of best brandy on the kitchen dresser was a life-saver! My mother together with her now surviving baby left her marriage-home with its three floors, including butcher's shop, its back facing the town slaughter house, for the safety and protection of my grandmother's home. But my father soon followed.

My father divided his time now between his market shop and the slaughter-house, where his passion for the task and his ambidexterity made him so good a slaughterman he was exempted from military service. Thus was his proficiency and skill in killing and cutting up cattle rewarded as war effort. In his shop in the market he contentedly cut up the meat but detested having to deal with the customers, usually my mother's role, his the procuring of cattle and other produce. He gambled a little though — mostly by various business methods made more money than he lost, and drank — though never to drunkenness — in the company of his market cronies. He seldom appeared at home, and as a child he seemed to me to be always 'up the market'. Whenever he came home he carried a pile of lamb chops or steak, which my mother was required to cook immediately, and which he rapidly ate then departed — 'up the market' again.

The market stall, where I had to spend many boring hours, I detested. The floor was covered with damp, soggy sawdust; the shelves were full of bloody and shapeless joints of meat; the walls were hung with the dripping carcasses of cattle; and there was an endless stream of chattering customers. There was nothing to play with except the knives and meat hooks; and everyone rushed around so, banging the door of the fridge, kicking up sawdust, and noisily tearing greaseproof paper, that there was neither joy nor peace. How I wished that my father kept a furniture, or grocery, or sweet shop, where the produce would be varied, interesting, and nice to touch and look at, not simply stinking carcasses and dripping blood. Sometimes a mountain sheep disappeared; and after slaughter in a nearby shed its skin was sold cheaply to the bewildered farmer.

My father's assistant Morgan, a kindly tubercular man, did most of the serving, charming the almost penniless customers with his friendly patter. This was the time of the Depression, and our stall sold the cheapest meat in the valley; and to hungry, unemployed families, a leg of lamb for a shilling, however inferior and unfit the meat, was preferable to no meat at all. My father was not given to questions on morality: he supplied the meat, and Morgan's eloquence sold it. The fat, shapeless women from up the far valleys, further in the mountains than I had ever been, arrived in torn, patched coats, shoes leaking in the continual Welsh rain, shopping with pennies and crowding the market each Friday. During the war meat was graded A and B, according to quality; the 'A' quality was kept for the special customers — my father, running a successful black market in butter, meat and poultry, had now built up a more respectable middle-class clientèle. The majority of customers were soon won over to Morgan's 'B for best' joints.

Johnny Starr, a sixty-year-old resilient West country man who always wore riding breeches, a black ankle-length braided top-coat in winter and summer, and carried a capacious wicker basket, delivered the meat throughout the valley. He would hover around the stall, teasing the fat, jelly-baby bosomed women, sweeping out the bloodied sawdust, and darting off with his laden basket, the Thersites of the market place. Whenever he visited a family where there'd been a birth that week he took a special 'A' piece of meat from his basket, saying only 'A split-arse or a young soldier?' as he jovially raised the celebratory glass offered. It was joked he slept with his daughter, and when teased, quipped that it was after her husband had left her so it didn't matter. He was always kind to me, bewildered and lost as I was in that rough male world.

It was Ted, one of my father's many cronies and hangers-on, who had the task of amusing me on those days there was no one at home to look after me. This care reached its peak one rain-sodden February day, when clothed in new black sou'wester and shiny mackintosh, I was visited by an urgent passion for a bucket and spade. Ted took me to Woolworths to get it. Then accoutred as I was for all storms, and joyously carrying a Mickey Mouse beach bucket and wooden spade, Ted was compelled to walk me for hours along the rainy shopping street of the town, to his discomfort, the amusement of his friends and passers-by — 'Going to build sand-castles, Ted?' — 'How about a ride across the sands on a donkey, Ted?', and to my total, perverse, oblivious joy. All the wet afternoon we tramped the soaked town, while my mother served in the dripping stall, and my father drank in the dry, gambling bar.

Facing our market shop was the stall of Meg the greengrocer, who came from Cardiff every Friday and Saturday to sell her fruit and vegetables. She was accompanied by her 'husband' Jim, a club-footed man, who assisted in the business, and each long Saturday evening, while we slowly disposed of the remaining cuts of meat to the last and poorest customers who awaited the final, cheapest hours of selling, we were entertained by their regular Saturday night quarrel, when Jim would take some vegetables and fruit of his own to a nearby empty stall for selling. And all through the darkening evening, under the flickering oil lamps, they would, between serving customers and shouting out their wares, yell abuse at each other.

'You needn't come back to Cardiff with me, you lazy bugger. You can look after yourself.'

'I've got a wife up the Cape,' retorted Jim, remembering the remote valley so-called seemingly because of its flourishing mining community. 'I'll go up there tidy. To hell with you, Meg Williams.'

'You're as rotten as your apples, you club-footed bastard,' continued Meg, now oblivious of the source of his produce.

'Soft pears for old mares,' retorted Jim, pointing a pear in her direction.

'You'd better take one for your cowing wife. It's all she's fit for,' retorted Meg.

Meg was the aunt of a Welsh boxer whose mother had died some years before her son's fame. After a few Guinnesses, and in a lull between customers, she would address the passing shoppers — 'He ought to go up the Rhondda to his mother's grave. There she is in the rain without a stone to cover her, love her. And not a flower ever. Up the Rhondda he ought to go! That's where the bugger ought to be! His mother's grave's a disgrace. Not a flower. Not one chipping — and him with all that money. It's a disgrace — what you want, dear, some gibbons?' and Meg adjourned her tirade to the market place while she served a customer.

And at nine o'clock prompt, friendship renewed, Meg and Jim would shut down their stalls and go off for a drink. She now talked of her boys at home, for at Meg's house the homeless boys, from bastardy or borstal, found a gruff welcome, a warm and rough love, secure in the judgment of her sharp tongue and big heart.

Like a breath of fresh air were the trips to 'the country', which meant the Carmarthenshire farms. The van was loaded with crates of whisky, hard to come by during the war, boxes of chocolates and various tinned foods, and I was placed in the back with these commodities, with my own ration of sweets and some promise of a new toy on return. We were welcomed at the farms on our route. As our supplies disappeared, the van was increasingly filled with vats of butter, crates of eggs, and, it seemed, hundreds of dead, furry rabbits, with staring eyes and each with its mark of blood.

At every farmhouse we were greeted by bounding, barking sheep dogs, excited by our butcher smells, and my father made his way to the living room of the farmhouse, where chickens, sometimes a lamb, dogs, and cats wandered about in ark-like amity. This was when, talking with the gruff farmers who had gathered for his visit, a bottle of whisky open on the table, and the red-faced farmer's wife cooking a meal on the open fire while expertly dodging and being dodged by the congregation of animals, my father was happiest, at home and at ease in the rough, direct farming life he had belonged to as a boy. These visits made money, but this, though he would never have admitted it even to himself, was not the main reason for his jaunts 'down the country'. Alas! pampered and indulged by the more feminine and intellectual tutelage of my grandmother, to my father's growing bitterness and contempt, I clearly showed an aversion to this earthy sensual life. His attempts in later years, by making me cut up meat and skin rabbits — a task I finally learned to do with some proficiency — to throw me in at the deep and bloody end simply changed my aversion to hostility. I found the farm boys, whose company I was sometimes left in, tough and crude, and remained afraid not only of the horse but the cow.

Some of my few happy memories, and ones of rare harmony, were returning on the trips on which my mother had accompanied us. I was spending one of my brief spells in the back of the van, loaded with sweets and chocolate and lost among the stiff, staring rabbits, the stacked butter and cheese, crates of eggs, and assorted poultry. I was placed there as the sleeping child for whose sake the policeman, should he stop us for one of those periodic war-time checks on travellers, could be dissuaded from opening the back of the van, thus disturbing me. The ruse must have proved successful, for though we were usually stopped at least once during the journey, I never recall the back door of the van being flung open, my seeming sleep disturbed for ever, and the illicit produce discovered to the world. In the front my mother seemed always to be singing, as the old van clanked through the black-out towns, villages, and countryside, 'There'll be blue-birds over the white cliffs of Dover' and as I eventually fell asleep among the staring eyes, the song promised some bright, comfortable morning. It was the early days of the war and the sense of threat and danger had entered, by a child's images and fantasy, even my own private world. One of the verses of this song told of how a little boy called Jimmy would one day sleep again in his own room. This puzzled me deeply, for Jimmy was the name of my playmate who lived next door and however often I questioned him he insisted he did sleep in his own room. Indeed, he regularly challenged me to a fight to prove it. But I chose not to fight, since he was the second best fighter in the street, and went on being puzzled.

The market stall was bordered by the river and since it was a patchwork wooden structure, was visited by the rats. They came at night, and with surgeon-like precision, would remove the kidneys from the hanging carcasses in the days before we owned a fridge, leaving no trace or mark of their visit on the carcass except the absent kidneys. Whoever first entered the shop in the morning was well advised to declare noisily his arrival, and allow any rats time to depart. One of my father's assistants, a courageous but sadistic young man, once surprised a rat, took up the meat chopper and cornered it in his private hunting expedition. The rat, evading the descending chopper, tore open the youth's leg, which became so poisonous with gangrene it had to be amputated. After that we looked on the kidneys as tribute money.

Friday, market-day, was the great occasion of the week and the stall became a club. The customers exchanged their gossip while they waited, and Morgan drank continuous bottles of Guinness while he served. In the thirties they begged and wheedled to have the joints for a penny less, and during the war to have a penny-worth more — 'not all that old corned beef'.

'I'm the man they couldn't bloody kill!' Morgan would frequently shout, beating his breast in triumph, after a brief but recuperative stay in the T.B. hospital. It was part of the Friday routine.

There was a small, shabbily though not poorly dressed woman who came each Friday, and waited her turn unspeaking, while she clutched a half crown in her palm with such a protective ferocity that I was sure she had so guarded it all the way from home. When her turn came she would thrust the coin on the counter and say simply 'Leg of lamb'. On some occasions there wasn't one available for that price, so that Morgan would have to say 'Sorry, love, but we haven't got one for 2/6 today. It'll cost two and ninepence.' At this she would nervously and helplessly push the silver coin forward on the counter, and declare feebly 'Leg of lamb, please. He won't give me any more. He only gives me 2/6.'

'Well, try tomorrow, love, we may have one then, about four o'clock.'

On Saturday afternoon the remainder of the meat was auctioned.

'Can't, I'll be in the flour. Can't — I'll be in the flour.'

Many months I wondered the meaning of this, and my imagination usually ended up picturing the woman groping, still clutching her 2/6, through a sea of flour. Later, on my inquiring, my mother explained that all day Saturday she would be baking the week's bread and *teisen lap* — a special Welsh cake.

On Thursday, anticipating the week-end, Aunty Martha would arrive, having just collected her widow's pension from the nearby post-office. On reaching the counter, she would first relate, in minute but dramatic detail, the odyssey of her journey from home to the market stall, whom she met on the way, what words of greeting or news they exchanged. After a few weeks I knew the outline by heart, and would look for news of the acquaintances she had met with the rapt and curious attention one awaits the happenings in a play. Her traveller's tale completed, Aunty Martha would take out her snuff box and offer Moses 'a pinch' with the comic-familiar and anticipated 'Put your finger in my hole, Mog, it's a bit of best brown Menthol.' On her arrival, of course, serving in the shop stopped, and we took our mid-morning rest. Morgan then produced a bottle of Guinness, which they shared, on either side of the counter, while Martha now proceeded to relate any major events in her life during the past week. If anyone at the back of the queue got restive during Martha's monologues and tried to edge forward 'Mind the goot!' called Morgan smiling, but firmly. 'Mind the goot, love!'

Early in the war her son Jenkyn, whom she always referred to fully as Jenkyn Davies, was called up, and his unexpected embarkation leave was her topic one lost, unforgettable Friday. Morgan was just pouring out the Guinness.

'Yesterday — it was just after the nine o'clock news, I was sitting on the lav at the bottom of the garden, eating a Jaffa. I heard somebody open the garden gate, so I put my Jaffa down on the lav seat. Then I heard his voice "Mam! It's me, where are you?" It was Jenkyn Davies! And before I had time to answer he'd opened the garden gate. Then into the lav he came. "What d'you want that rubbish for?" He said, pointing at the Jaffa on the seat, "Come on up 'The Lamb' for a drink, Mam!" So up "The Lamb" we went': Aunty Martha's face beamed with joy, 'and we drank till the ashes filled the grate — we met the men on the morning shift on the way home!' She took a sip from her Guinness — 'Have you got something special for Jenkyn Davies's dinner, Mog? I'll have my Sunday joint I think, as he's going tomorrow. I told him, if he goes to France he must visit his father's grave. Funny thing but William Davies has been calling me a lot these last few weeks.' Morgan produced a succulent joint of Welsh lamb — and another Guinness. Nobody seemed in a hurry to be served.

Not even grief robbed Aunty Martha of her gift for narrative, for one Thursday some months later, telling of Jenkyn's death at Dunkirk she related how 'on Monday morning I was just taking the top off my egg when the telegram came'. And in the manner of her way of understanding there was sorrow in her voice, but no tears or complaint, only humility before life. And although her living would never be the same again, she had first gone through the ritual story of those she had met, offered her snuff, and taken her first sip of the Guinness before relating her tragedy.

With immediate, instinctive kindness Morgan tried to provide an extra special joint for women whose husbands or sons were briefly at home on leave, and my father would produce a small parcel of butter, eggs and sugar, so that blackmarketeering seemed an inappropriate term for the exchange and mart in rationed foods, that he took such joy in running — a joy that derived more from the excitement than any marginal profit that remained at the end of the long process of exchange and barter.

During the war, of course, except on Friday and Saturday when the available meat was distributed, the shop was seldom open longer than the morning hours. On Tuesday, for corned beef; Wednesday, for tripe and sausages; Thursday, for rabbits from the country. Yet, though each week usually brought some story of personal grief, there was not that despair, that hopelessness that was so much part of the atmosphere, and so vivid 'up the market', during the impoverished thirties.

By this time, though as usual I hated it, it was my job to assist in the making of sausages every Tuesday in a nearby shed. Scraps of meat, flabby, slippery white tripe — whose slimy sponge-like touch I still remember — and bloodied-purple lights, were stacked ready for the giant mincing machine; nearby were emptied corned beef tins, greasy and with sharp, jagged edges, full of congealed blood to add to the mixture — particularly for making black pudding. The only thing I didn't detest was the soya flour. It was my job to pile the mixture into the mincing machine; and to append, at the other end where the soggy mass eventually emerged, the long, salt-covered skins. On sausage-making day they lay in a pile like giant, soiled condoms. I soon tired of turning the machine handle, and the art of tying the yards of distended sausage into finger-length sizes I never really mastered. Yet, next to the gossiping drama of the customers in the shop, this was the part of being a butcher I liked best. There was something of a craft in making the sausages, there was machinery to control and with the exception of the tins of blood, the items one had to use seemed more like materials, and somewhat removed from the immediate distaste and disgust that the carcasses hanging in the shop, ready for cutting up, aroused.

Once only did I accompany my father to the slaughterhouse to observe his expert butchery, and the years of late childhood and early adolescence were haunted by the cries and sight of the sheep, their throats slit, bleeding to death, while my father unskinned those ahead in the dying queue. Perhaps I was too squeamish, perhaps his efforts to involve me in his trade were too unthinking; certainly the consequence was a rooted, instinctive hostility and a reversion to more gentle, feminine, humane worlds.

The best morning was Sunday morning, the day my parents stayed late in bed, and I was allowed to amuse myself with the paper bags of copper and silver coins that had not yet been taken to the bank. For hours I rolled them along the floor, no doubt losing the odd coin; but it did not matter as there were so many. Due no doubt to this game, I always thought of coins simply as toys, things to be played with — there always seemed to be plenty around. On days when the rag-and-bone man, with his frail horse and cart, came down the street calling for old clothes, I immediately began a frantic search through the household for discarded clothes. But should Caradoc offer in exchange, for I was a prized and regular customer, a few coppers, these I immediately flung in contempt at his feet, startling the sleepy horse with my anguish. I would make it clear I desired a piece of the china ware stacked in a grubby box on the cart. With relief, I would be presented, to my boundless joy, with a huge white mug or plate. It would be my heart's delight for the week, kept in a special place on the dresser in the kitchen, for my exclusive use at meal-times, and trusted only to my loving care during the dish-washing.

My other favoured toys from up the market were the small copper cartridges of which my father had large stocks for killing cattle. Flung about the oilcloth-covered floor, particularly when there was Friday's supply of coinage as well, there was enormous fun to be had with them as counters, soldiers, and a means of representation for all kinds of childish fantasy. The gun I ignored: it bored and rather frightened me. I would see it safely stored in another room, safe from any errant cartridges or the foolhardy fingers of my friends.

However, there was a real war going on at home, and once I grabbed the poker from the grate and attempted to hit my father who was attacking my mother in the back kitchen, but it was a child's ineffectual protest. Pushed aside I ran up the street to the pub, seeking the love and safety of my grandmother and her drinking companions.

The Kitchen Friends

The Lamb Inn stood at the top of the street, and in the kitchen, a half public, half private room of the pub, my grandmother held court. She would leave home each day at two, after my grandfather had left for the afternoon shift at the colliery, return at four thirty, since closing time was ostensibly four o'clock, and set out again at seven-thirty prompt for the evening session. Titus Evans, the landlord, respected and feared my grandmother, and she enjoyed the complete freedom of the pub. His wife, Gwen, was equally devoted to her, and their day seemed to revolve around her comings and goings. Family and friends addressed her as 'Mama', and she moved about her world with matriarchal authority. My father dubbed it 'Hell's kitchen'.

Titus and Gwen lived in the small back kitchen, which actually served as kitchen, dining room, and sitting room for them. Leading off was the pantry, with a small window onto the street: this was most important since my grandmother, or any others of her set, would beat at that window, should the back yard gate, by which they usually gained admittance to the back door of the pub, be inadvertently shut. At that sound Titus would rush, dropping whatever task was in hand, as though the Angel Gabriel himself were demanding admission. The middle room, called the kitchen and where 'the Kitchen friends' drank, always boasted, even in high summer, an open fire. It was furnished, like most sitting rooms of the time in this mining valley, with a variety of surprisingly comfortable wooden, but cushioned armchairs placed near the fire-place, a large old-fashioned table covered with a plush cloth, and at the far end some high-backed chairs used only by strangers who entered this privileged haven by mistake, and seldom entered again. It required several years' regular attendance to become a kitchen friend.

Beyond the kitchen lay the bar, an oblong room, with an

anthracite stove in the centre, much like the bar room of a Western, remarkably uncomfortable, with its few benches and rough, rather dirty tables, and used only by men. Its life really began about three o'clock, as the miners called in for a quick pint, after the morning shift, to wash away the coal dust. Bets were placed, the *Daily Herald* or *Daily Worker* studied in detail — especially the political and sporting pages — and arguments tentatively started that really flared in the long evenings over endless pints of smooth, pellucid Welsh bitter. It was as exclusively male as a St James's Club. Not even my grandmother had drunk there — those paying court came to her in the kitchen — and though I was a regular visitor to the kitchen from the time I could be carried in a shawl, I was twenty before I braved the bar. At the front of the pub was the large, plush, dusty, and never used Commercial Room: at Christmas and bank holidays an enormous coal fire (as most of the customers were miners coal was the one plentiful commodity in the street) roared and crackled there — quite alone apart from the occasional courting couple who came in out of the night and the cold.

In the kitchen my grandmother's was the corner armchair, between the fireplace and the window ledge, which sported a frail fern in a large green pot decorated on the outside with large, bulbous roses. The poor fern was permanently intoxicated for its pot was the surreptitious dumping ground of years of my mother's whiskies and gins. She enjoyed the company of the kitchen friends, and her own mother's patronage there, but simply did not like the taste of drink. And although almost ashen in colour, I cannot recall the fern dying.

The kitchen friends had a caste system that would have impressed even the Hindus, measured outwardly in the proximity of one's armchair to my grandmother's and the fireplace; but with implications much deeper, determining the value and validity of what one had to say, one's worth — social and moral — and in what order Gwen or Titus would serve the half of bitter that came in endless day and night rounds.

Aunty Martha, my grandmother's greatest boozing pal together with her daughters, had been even while I was a child, 'a widow these twenty years' and together with the usual seasonal and birthday festivities, the anniversary of the death of her husband William Davies was firmly in the kitchen boozing calendar. Such was her devotion to his memory that each Saturday night, occasional men friends notwithstanding, she would stand at 9.30 to declare 'I wouldn't marry another bloody man! Never! Not if he had balls of gold and his cock was studded with diamonds.' After which, with great dignity, she would resume her seat and order another round. At this point one of her friends, Benji, would delicately lift one trouser leg, and pointing at his hairless flesh say 'Look, like a lily, like a lily!' 'Ben's very tidy,' commended Martha, raising her glass. 'They always called him Ben Tidy as a young man. Shit! He'd shit in a teapot!' she concluded proudly. Occasionally he would spend the week-end with Aunty Martha, in her shoe-shaped corner house halfway down the street. After a quarrel he would leave quickly, a plate of apple tart, an offering he always brought, flying after him from the bedroom window.

My two aunts, Polly and Mary, were also of the kitchen friends. Polly at this time lived in the London suburb of Eltham, driven into unwilling exile in the thirties when her husband, a cheerful and innocuous collier, could find no work, and after twelve years on the dole migrated to 'work on the buildings' in London. But three or four times a year Aunty Polly, scrimping ha'pennies and pennies in a capacious china pot, that seemed to me as a child a treasure hoard, would have the fare to come home. The kitchen friends would go into beery and continuous conclave for days. Then on the afternoon of departure, she would call for a last farewell glass. Of course, she never left. Weekly this valedictory ceremony would take place till she had stayed the three months her rail ticket permitted. Consequently the exile was more her gentle husband's than her own. Aunty Mary, who lived in the next street, was daily in attendance in the intervals between caring for her miner husband and her children. She, alone, smoked and I remember her son, my close friend in these childhood years, confessing to me how sad he was he wasn't a girl so that when he grew up he could drink and smoke like a woman, too. All the husbands, but one, worked in the pits, drank only at weekends, were gentle, patient men who gladly handed over their pay packets and all household and family responsibility on Friday, then were doled out their pocket money, and were happy.

My mother set off in the morning to sell all day in our market stall the meat my father procured and butchered. So left in the care of my grandmother, before I had properly learned to crawl on all fours I was taken to the afternoon session up 'The Lamb'. Being a determined child, and preferring from birth brandy to milk, a measure was bought for me each afternoon, and my dummy was dipped in the glass from time to time — perhaps explaining why I was so reluctant to surrender this delicious teat even at the age of seven. I spent many hours pulling at the green plush cloth on the table, learning with its aid first to crawl, then to walk, and later to take cover. For occasionally a burly policeman, led off his beat by some inexplicable whim, would appear after closing time in the bar, and at the merest hint from Titus I would expertly nip under the table, safely hidden behind the voluminous plush, jealously guarding my unfinished brandy and the partly consumed glasses of beer also quickly hidden there. Meanwhile the bobby listened with increasing awe to the stories of the now beerless kitchen friends, while Gwen prepared a pot of tea and fancy cakes in her back kitchen. Gwen had aspirations to gentility and looked forward to these rare occasions when the ladies would join her in afternoon tea. As she appeared, with her laden tea-tray, the policeman retreated, humbled and confused.

Of course there were sad times, with their own appropriate ceremonies, as when one of the kitchen friends died. Then they would meet, dressed in black, and the window that looked onto the street, which was of frosted glass and usually closed against the stares and malicious gossip of the teetotal but so curious families, would be opened. A glass of beer placed on the sill for the 'departed friend' was ceremonially passed among the women to be sipped as the hearse passed outside.

And then the life went on.

One of the friends, Mam Jones, kept a shop in her front room. Though shop was rather a grand word, and the room seemed always to be dark, untidy, and not very clean. Even to childhood eyes, the few bottles of boiled sweets, the box of spanish root, a few loaves of bread, a box of Mars Bars and Choconuts, bottles of pop and vinegar and slabs of salt seemed sparse merchandise. The craze for spanish root, a fibrous liquorice-root, came and went inexplicably. For weeks everyone would be chewing spanish root and gobbing the masticated remains in the street — not a pear drop nor minto, liquorice toffee nor pepsin, never even yellow sherbet, was to be seen for days. Mam Jones's speciality was laverbread and cockles on Friday, when she would journey by bus, carrying capacious black oilcloth bags, to collect from Swansea Market. It gave special excitement to Friday's dinner. And on Tuesdays she made faggots and peas, that you could buy on the book, for she seemed to have an endless supply of these small, cloth-bound ledgers, that, to our eyes, gave tick and charity like some beneficent Bible. 'Tell your mother to pay me on Friday, when she comes for cockles,' she'd declare, for when food was wanted on tick the kids were sent — an always observed though unwritten rule of commerce.

One of our greatest pleasures when we had no money for sweets, was to watch Mam Jones's departure in the late afternoon to 'The Lamb', for then we knew her husband, an ancient man with a lined, wizened face and grey walrus moustache, would be sitting alone in the back kitchen. He never left the kitchen, except to go out the back to the lavatory or upstairs to bed. We would enter the doorway of the front room shop, which was never closed or locked, and shout 'Shop! Shop! Shop!' At first there would be silence. Then, as our calls of 'Shop!' continued, a voice would growl from the kitchen 'There's nobody in!'

After each cry of 'Shop' would come the reply, 'There's nobody in!' After several minutes of this exchange her husband would add to the reiterated reply of 'There's nobody in! — She's up "The Lamb!"'

'Shop!'
'There's nobody in! She's up "The Lamb"!'
'Shop!'
'There's nobody in! She's up "The Lamb"!'
'Shop!'
'There's nobody in! She's up "The Lamb"!'

We never received a different reply, nor did Mr Jones ever emerge from the kitchen, nor relapse into silence. So after half an hour of this, we got tired, and ran off to play a different game.

After Mam Jones died, on a bleak February day in the first year of the war, due to a severe fall coming home one night down the strangely darkened street of the blackout, we still called at the shop nobody bothered to empty or shut. But however often we rapped our pennies on the counter and called, the only reply we got from the back kitchen was 'There's nobody in! There's nobody in!'

And the childwood we called unknowingly to re-enter was already dead too.

The Street

Until I joined the gang, my relations with the street where I lived were, like those of my family, tentative, proud, inhibited. As my father was in business we were financially more secure, and enjoyed a higher standard of living than most; we were also as a family more private in our way of life and largely rejected the communal life of the street. This tendency was increased by my grandmother's devotion to the local, for the more respectable women neighbours were critical of the ladies who met daily there. They hugged their respectability and their pride, while we, mostly indifferent, were busily enjoying our less conventional household, confident in our more independent way of life. Yet neither side of the family — my grandmother's independent, intellectual, political and lapsed Nonconformist tradition, nor my father's farming and small town businessman's position — aspired to middle-class habits and a house in the posh, professional part of the town on West Hill.

My instinctive nervousness of the rough boys of the neighbourhood was fostered by the over-protective attitude of the household, an upbringing more cocooned financially and culturally than the tougher life of the street. There was, until schooldays, a reluctance for me to mix with the street that I too readily accepted. Before schooldays, my explorations into the street were mostly accompanied by my grandmother or grandfather; in the afternoon my grandmother and I would stroll down to the river bank, often only to view the sluggish stream and deposit our daily bucket of ashes and rubbish onto the piles of garbage that cluttered the bank. What a monstrous breach of freedom it seemed when, after the war, garbage was daily collected and surreptitious disposal of rubbish into the river was prosecuted — if we were caught by the infrequent patrolling policeman. But it seemed to me such a waste of time, especially when involved in such rubbish-compiling tasks as tidying the garden, to leave the tins of junk and stones on the roadside for collection rather than make the quick expedition of carting them down to the river. Often as children we awaited patiently the arrival of junk and rubbish, and investigated it with predatory delight — often discovering useful boxes, the odd wheel — even a battered pram or a tyre on occasion, bed-springs, a mattress for the den, interesting items of broken china, strange shapes of metal, and the endless, esoteric treasure of boys.

The last excitement of the day was the stroll down to the river at midnight with my grandfather, after he had eaten his supper, drunk his flagon of beer and I had slowly, cherishing each mouthful, drunk the remaining water in his jack. At this time, with only the light of the stars or the moon, and the steady humming of the water audible in the quiet of night, the riverside, its cluttered banks assuming strange shapes and qualities, was at its most attractive. On the far side the line of trees and bushes that grew at the water's edge cast moving shadows, and beyond the mountains reared.

I was the proud but ineffective possessor of a three-wheeled Mickey Mouse bike, also a red motor car; alas, neither of these did I ever entirely master. On occasions when I played with them in the street I was soon surrounded by friends also eager to try them out. And they did this expertly — especially Freddie, who lived next door. Sooner or later the toy was damaged and I retreated in tears, tears usually aggravated by a fight to regain control of my vehicle, a fight I usually lost on points; for though I lacked aggressive fists I was quite good at defending myself. If really goaded and I let fly a hard jab, I would soon run away before the stunned fighter assumed a more vicious style. On one occasion only I really lost my temper, when Freddie kept cheating playing marbles, and finally demanded my best taws — the larger marbles we used to make our shots. I kept my store of marbles in a cotton flour bag and, enraged, began to flay Freddie on the back with the bag. At first too surprised to hit back, and soon too hurt to wish to, Freddie went home crying to fetch his big brother, Johnnie. Seizing the opportunity I rushed home, banging the front door securely behind me. After such battles I would retreat into home company for days, abandoning the street. On that occasion, each day for a week, Freddie would violently kick our front door every morning when passing — and my grandmother was never in time to catch him.

After a losing battle, especially if I retired with signs of blood, and as my nose bled very easily this was often, I was at once comforted if my grandmother would go to the front door and shout abuse at the offending victor. This verbal retaliation from a member of the loser's family was part of the ritual of our street fights, and the victor with the rest of the gang would thereupon run away to the safety of our den. If blood was shed on both sides, both families sometimes harangued in the street — to the awe and righteous pleasure of the original contestants, who usually resumed friendship the same day.

My closest relationship was with my cousin, who was a year younger and lived in the next street. I often joined his own street friends who were fewer in number and more interested in playing games than we were. Consequently the boys in my street thought me treacherous, not to be entirely trusted. At the times of retreat into family life I spent much time, accompanied by my cousin, playing in the small tent we erected in the garden. We were enviously watched, from the garden fence, by both the gangs we had rejected. We mounted guard near the tent, for sooner or later we would be attacked, usually after dark.

Alone of the family, I cared for the garden, with passionate, eager, though intermittent, bouts of industry. But however much rubbish I carted away during these periods, carefully planting grass seeds, nasturtiums and sunflowers — for I knew only the hardiest plants had any chance there — in due course the garden would become the dumping ground for household rubbish and junk, especially in winter months, and my efforts were regularly thwarted. But the rose bush blossomed each summer, despite weeds and waste, and near it, with full ceremony, my cousin as undertaker, myself as priest, we buried each of our cats. As we always kept two, and a cat's life was particularly hazardous owing to the poison laid for them in the nearby allotments, a burial was necessary from time to time. Afterwards we had a solemn tea, and went to the pictures.

Stan, an old miner who lived next door, kept chickens, and the brick wall that ran along one side of the garden formed part of the chicken shed. He allowed his chickens to wander about his yard and the lane that ran along the bottom of the gardens. Our garden was the Mecca for his scratching, squawking fowls, for they always found their way there, assisted by the ease with which they could squeeze through the unevenly placed and rough wooden spars that made up our garden gate. In any case the gate was often left open. It seemed to me as they scratched at my beloved seeds, and trampled my weakly plants, that to pelt them with all available small stones and missiles, so that the garden became one squawking battle ground as the hens were finally driven back through the gate, was a just retaliation. Arguments flared between Stan and my grandmother as to the propriety of this action, but the hens continued to invade, and I continued to hurl my ineffective deterrents.

One November 5th my cousin and I decided on a private bonfire in the garden. The relative merits of the various bonfires in the neighbourhood were measured by the number of old car tyres each had acquired.

'How many tyres you got?'

'We got six. We raided two from the "Crown Arabs".'

'They set our bonfire on fire last Friday. So we had to start again.'

'Our stuff is in Freddie's shed, and his dog is guarding it.'

'Have you got a guy?'

'Not yet. But Uncle Graham is making one.'

The street bonfires became a social occasion, visited by gossiping women and curious fathers. Few of us could afford many fireworks, so the bonfire was the centre of excitement. My father had supplied eight tyres for our private pyre, so ours, especially in the narrow confines of the garden, was phenomenal. He also left us half a gallon of petrol as an incentive to the flames at the beginning of the blaze.

It provided a marvellous conflagration, from the very moment when the first petrol-sodden flames leapt and curled about the pillar of tyres; lighting the neighbourhood of land and sky, its glow reddened even the river, fifty yards away. But at such close quarters, Stan's hens began to squawk and cackle at the increasing heat. Already the brick walls of the chicken shed were too hot to touch, and the smell of burning rubber filled the air. Soon Stan appeared on the scene, protesting at the so narrowly confined conflagration. My grandmother was ready for him: she was tired of the predatory chickens, and a few days previously one of Stan's nomadic geese, visiting our garden in ferocious inquisition, had pecked her while she was fetching a bucket of coal from the coalhouse. Stan soon retreated, able at least to release his chickens into the redly glowing relative coolness of his smoky backyard. 'Stan, I'm kilt! I'm kilt!' cried his wife from their back kitchen.

At this stage I was in many ways a wilful child, and this wilfulness was, when it seemed beneficial, encouraged by the family. But of course it had its less social occasions. If refused anything I desired, I usually reacted by threatening some kind of retaliation — usually the destruction of a pane of coloured glass in the ornate glass door in the passageway. I cannot recall that this particular threat was ever fulfilled. However, another took a more curious, involved form of persuasion. One of my constant, and always refused demands, was for a dog. On this particular day we had just had tinned salmon for tea. The used, jagged-edged tin was on the floor, in shining emptiness, since the cat had licked away the few oily remains offered, and was purring contentedly on the mat before the sweating coal fire. My mother and grandmother were gossiping, joined by my favourite aunt who always wore black. It was a beautiful summer day, and from the mountains gently climbed blue skies. Next door Gyp was barking excitedly — no doubt Freddie was about to take him walking.

'If I can't have a dog like Gyp I — I,' I spied the salmon tin and picked it up, 'I'm going to throw this salmon tin through next door's back kitchen window.'

The gossiping women took little notice. It was an esoteric threat.

'If I can't have a dog like Gyp I'm going to throw this salmon tin through next door's back kitchen window.'

The women still talked. 'Try the glass door,' said my mother in sarcastic aside.

I walked out to the backyard where beyond a brick wall a little higher than myself was next door's large kitchen window. I flung the tin. It sailed over the wall and out of sight. Silence. Then a splintering of glass.

After the row I was sent to bed.

Coming downstairs in the evening, slowly, nervously, the bottom stair creaked, and the door at the bottom of the stairs was clipped. I knocked faintly. Then, fearfully, louder. After an anxious minute my grandmother opened the door. She said nothing, but let me in — and winked. My mother, unspeaking, scowled in the kitchen. My grandmother put the tongs into the red coals, preparatory to curling her hair.

'I'll go up a bit earlier to catch Jinny. She usually goes at nine. I'll ask her if Reuben can put the glass in tomorrow.'

'Can I come up Gran?' My tone was wistful.

'Certainly not. You've done enough damage for one day.' My mother glared. She was frying chops, obviously my father was expected soon. 'There'll be no pocket money for a month. And you can't go to Freddie's party either.'

'He may as well come up. He can help me me carry the flagon back. Get your coat on.' This time there was no dissent from my mother.

I put on my coat sheepishly.

And set off joyfully.

The usual ladies were gathering in the kitchen.

'Has Jinny been in?' my grandmother asked.

'She's due any time now,' Gwen replied, fetching my grandmother a glass of beer. I sat quietly in the corner. Reuben Hughes, Jinny's husband, was a 'potcher'; that is, he did odd household jobs in his rough and ready but usually effective way. He did not charge very much. And nobody in our community would think of having a job done professionally — since there were plenty of potchers among the unemployed who would do most jobs for a few shillings — and there was no point in jeopardising the money one didn't have. Practising these many small skills went by the name of hobbling. My grandmother related the story, and bought me a glass of pop. I sat delighted, almost a hero.

'Of course Reuben'll mend the window,' said Jinny, on arrival. 'He'll be down tomorrow — first thing.' My grandmother bought her a glass. 'It's about time the old bugger did something,' she added.

At the end of the night the ladies decided to go home with Jinny, each armed with a flagon, and headed by my grand mother, to give Reuben the message. The winged messengers deliberated on their supply of beer.

'I'll just get a flagon of mild for Reuben,' said Jinny.

'Take this flagon home and tell your mother I'm going down to Jinny's about the window.'

'Can I come too?'

'If your mother's willing.'

I ran down with the flagon. My mother was in the kitchen, crying. There had been a fight with my father, who had as so often now left in a temper. Gugga would be in soon, and my mother was putting his bucket of bath water onto the fire.

'You can go if you like. I'm going to bed soon.'

I raced back to the pub.

In Jinny's house the boozing party was soon under way. By midnight only Reuben's flagon was left.

'Well, I'm not waiting much longer for the old bugger', said Jinny. 'He's been out since dinner time.' The beery women eyed the remaining flagon greedily. Jinny's huge black cat Whisky was sleeping in my lap, and I was sitting on the fender by the fire reading my grandmother's John Myers goods catalogue. From time to time the women filed out, 'I must have a pee, love.'

'Just go in the kitchen by there. There's a bowl on the floor ready. It's too far to walk up the garden to the lav.'

Till midnight I listened to the tales of the clucking women, often pretending to be asleep if their reminiscences were salty.

Soon Reuben's flagon was opened.

'What about Reuben?' inquired one of the women, pricked by sudden conscience.

'I know — we'll top it up from the bowl,' joked Jinny.

As we were bidding goodnight, Reuben appeared, a tall gaunt man wearing earrings and with a hare-lip. He had lived once as a Gypsy, and sometimes missed that life now that he had settled down to live with Jinny. Jinny's husband had been killed in the war, and the record of his sacrifice hung in a shiny black frame above the mantelpiece. Reuben greeted the women jovially. Then they all walked home along the river bank, cursing the dark and the need to get up at four o'clock to put the men off for the morning shift. I clutched a small brass ring, a lucky charm Reuben had given me.

The next morning Reuben came to mend the window. I carried my lucky charm for a fortnight.

Often, especially on warm summer Saturday nights when the neighbours found their drama and release in family brawls, the street fights became communal. These were much more exciting than the quarrels at home, when I listened in bed to the shouting and bitter cries of my mother and father from the kitchen below and wished only that they would end. Our family conducted their wars at home; they were private, personal; more claustrophobic in consequence. But with most families — especially in many cases related families, usually parents and married children, sharing a six-roomed house with one kitchen and lavatory (nobody in our neighbourhood had a bathroom) — the conflicting passions, when the fighting began, needed a bigger stage. So the family, led usually by the two men in combat, filed into the street, for though it might begin as a women's quarrel, the final stage usually involved the husbands.

Then there would be a fight in the street, when fists flew, and the aroused and still rather drunk protagonists were egged on and championed by the women and children of their own immediate family, for usually of course the contestants were related, since the street consisted largely of half a dozen inter-marrying families. To do their courting youngsters seldom went more than a few doorsteps away, for the neighbourhood atmosphere was propitious and friendly to love-making in the half-dark. Inevitably, brought to the surface by beer, hidden enmities and resentments held back during the crowded, busy and congested course of domestic events in the week, exploded on Saturday nights. But the next day everything was as proper as Sunday.

Rather distinctive were the marital battles of our pub neighbours. The husband, a very hard-working collier, was a cheerful, humorous, rather easy-going man, with a bald head. It seemed unsurprising that his hair refused to grow, for when they quarrelled his red-haired Irish wife would aim at his head the nearest piece of china given to them by his mother, and originally these were many, since his mother's delight was collecting items of china and various pieces were passed over to them to make way for the new. Brigid was of quick, but soon-forgiving temper, and in turn the wall-plates of Lord Roberts and Kitchener, the Victoria and Albert tea-set, and a slender ornate glass vase all came to grief, hitting the wall as Eddie ducked his shining bald pate. Eddie would plead mercy for himself and the china gifts of his mother, could never hit his wife, but became skilled at ducking and shielding his head with his hands. Finally only the po with pink roses on remained, secure, it seemed, under the bed. But one Saturday night in Spring it went hurtling towards his head. Eddie ducked, and the po crashed through the window and fell, splintering into the street, narrowly missing the constable on his night beat.

Everything was right as rain in the morning.

It was soon after the salmon tin incident that our neighbours moved to London in search of work, settling in rooms in Kennington. They gave their cat to friends in the next street, but though pelted by the new inhabitants it kept coming back to the now unwelcoming house. A stray I sometimes fed, it kept its loyalty to the house next door, however stoned and incomprehensible its feline exile.

The Gang

With the advent of Freddie as leader the gang turned outward, became nomadic. Though our den remained at the bottom of the street, near the river, we made expeditions to other parts of the neighbourhood. They began as exploratory, but on meeting other gangs, they became hostile in intent and predatory by nature. Freddie was the proud owner of a magnificently tough mongrel, called Gyp, and Gyp usually went ahead of the gang, sniffing and barking, lean and loyal. At games of cricket, an agile fielder, he leapt and caught the ball in his jaws. When the ball was hit into the river, a boundary, he dived into the water and retrieved it, wagging his dripping tail as he clambered in triumph up the bank. He was a fearless Cerberus in the falling dusk when candle-ends lit the stumps and we battled on beside the darkening stream.

Our great rivals, and sworn enemies most of the time, were the 'Crown Arabs', who roved the slag-tips and the nearby mountain-side. They were a glamorous and fierce gang. Mostly they went to the nearby tin church, so called because of its structure of corrugated iron sheets painted a dark red, quite unlike the familiar grey stone and guardian chapels. They were tough, but less brutal than ourselves, and much preoccupied with roving the mountainside, hunting for rabbits and grass snakes, and fishing for trout in the mountain streams, rather romantic gypsy-like adventurers. They all lived near the pub called 'The Crown', while our parents frequented 'The Lamb', excellent reasons for childhood rivalry. The gang's name 'The Crown Arabs' was inherited from the name given to the local pub jazzband during the 1926 strike, when jazzbands were popular in the mining valleys.

The climax of our enmity came with a calculated and system-atised battle of the snakes. It took place on a hot July day, when the grass snakes were innocently basking in the sun, among the patches of fern. Battle was not joined until each of our leaders had a grass snake looped from his hand, and first entered the fray, symbolically hurling their captive snakes at each other. The snakes soon scuttled away, forgotten in the excitement of the fight. I was matched against a dark gypsy-like boy, nicknamed Micky, lithe and gentle in his movements, as disinclined to fisticuffs as myself, and ours became more a loving tussle until the arrival of the ice cream van diverted all attention from the pitched battle. After we'd all eaten a cornet somehow the hostility was melted, and we decided to separate into two football teams instead. But I didn't like football, so at Micky's invitation, for he seemed equally uninterested in the game, we went off to look for trout in the mountainside streams.

But no such friendships or descents into amity were permitted or even contemplated, in our fierce, daily and unremitting battles with the Catholic boys. These fights were waged with all the passion, ruthlessness, and savagery of religious wars. No quarter was given, or expected. The set battles were regularly occasioned by the fact that the Catholics had to come to our school to receive their school dinners — so were they not eating *our* food in *our* canteen? Of course we didn't question this — it was ordained, presumably, by our Headmaster, and therefore though inexplicable was as inevitable as the laws of nature.

At the lower end of our street, along the course of the brook, ran a wire fence which, as the wires were each a foot apart, it was easy to get through, though a too hasty and unpractised scurry through the fence could mean wet feet from slipping into the brook, a hazard that, in the joy of battle, hardly concerned anyone. On the other side of the brook reared the high grassy bank, and on top of this ran the railway line. Now the tougher, more daring, and adventurous Catholic boys chose not to walk along the main road to our school for their lunch, but to take a short cut through the gasworks, along the railway line, down the slippery bank, and across the brook. Their outward journey to our school was uneventful, since we were at the first sitting, ravenously eating. It was on the return journey that passions flared, friendships were made and lost, and the brief skirmishes were enjoyed by all.

After the death of Duggie, who alone had the nerve to charge up the grassy bank in the face of hurtling stones, whoever first held the railway line won the battle honours, for the railway track was laid with small stones and rubble — a heaven-sent armoury! Over school dinner the excitement would suddenly become palpable, the sweet was rushed, the girls chattered indifferently, and the message 'let's guard the railway line!' was passed from table to table. Sometimes the 'Crown Arabs' joined us, but they were fickle in allegiance.

As in cold-war tactics, any excuse for annoying the other side was found — a verbal insult, the stealing of a school cap, a planned pushing of the awaiting line of second-sitting diners as we left the canteen. We seldom declared hostilities without feigned reason or due warning. Our strategy was then to get up on to the railway line, and make convenient piles of stones for the forthcoming charge. Sometimes, if important members of the gang had to run errands, we didn't make the railway line; often, too, the passing of a train, and the consequent dangers of prosecution if we were caught near the line, forced us to run helter-skelter down the bank, our ammunition abandoned and exposed to the charge of stones hurtling from below, the missiles grabbed from the brook, while the slow moving train passed from sight.

It was the strategy of those below in the street to take partial cover in doorways, or behind the sheds, while the stones hurtled down, darting out to grab one and throw it back at an opportune moment. The hail of stones back and forth would continue until the time for afternoon school stopped hostilities or someone was struck and hurt, for the drawing of blood, as by some sacrificial rite, brought reconciliation and a quick end to the charge. Often a stone would sail through someone's front window, and a second after the splintering crash not a boy would be visible on the line or in the street, while the gathering group of angry neighbours prepared to clout the likely combatants at home. My only scar, on the head and where the hair still refuses to grow, was earned not in these gang conflicts. It happened when inexplicably and violently the street-wise tomboy girl I used to play with hit me one winter's day with the shovel we were using to clear the snow from the pavement. I bled profusely. Once there was serious injury, when my friend Jimmy lost an eye, and there were stern reprimands from the Headmaster, and a policeman awesomely patrolled the line for a few days. But the stone charges and battles continued, even if we had to go farther afield for combatants.

It was the river bank that provided most of our adventures, and especially exciting were the occasions when the local council would, with publicity and ceremony, decide the river should be filled with minnows and trout to encourage some river-life. We innocently watched while a Councillor, with due gravity, performed the ceremony. The fish duly deposited, the Councillor and his attendants departed, after congratulating themselves on their performance with a few speeches on the social benefits supplied by a council mindful of its civic duties.

We watched the departure of the last of the council delegation, then proceeded to our section of the riverbank to await the arrival of the celebrated, unsuspecting fish! The next few days were devoted to tickling trout, which we cooked over fires on the bankside under the railway bridge. It was a time when feet were often cut on bits of china and glass when paddling in the river, and we were more often wet than dry.

By the afternoons our minds turned from fishing to exploring the refuse on the stretch of bank used for rubbish. The discovery of a bedspring meant that for a few days, having torn the springs from the mattress and tied one to each of the soles of our shoes, we went clumsily springing about in short, exhausting jumps, and so ran errands, fought, wandered, played our games.

Our favourites were kick-a-tin and follow-the-leader. For kick-a-tin, we placed an old tin can in a circle drawn with a stick on the stony dirt-track that served as roadway in the street. The last to arrive on the scene, while preparations were in progress, acted as 'man'. The leader of the rest ran towards the tin and gave it a hefty kick from the ring. The moment his boot hit the tin the rest of us ran in search of a hide-out, while the poor fellow who was 'man' had to fetch the tin, replace it in the ring, and make an agreed count (usually fifty or hundred) aloud before he could come in search of us. Having caught sight of us, no doubt inadvertently peeping from a splendid hide-out in someone's hen coop, pig-sty, or back-shed, the name of the recognised person would be called while he raced back to the ring. If he kicked the tin first that person was 'caught' and waited near the ring. If the recognised person won the race to the ring and kicked the tin first, any already 'caught' were released and the poor wretch who was 'man' began the procedure all over again. However, should someone inadvertently kick the tin before anyone had been called or caught he replaced the 'man' as the wretched hunter, and the former joyously rejoined the rest of the gang in search of a hiding place. Often, especially in the half-dark of evening, the tin was kicked by someone while the 'man' went searching for the rest of the gang, so that his prisoners were once more released. And the 'man' went through the procedure again and again, until we tired of the game or he went home in despair. Often we became so enamoured of our latest hide-out that we stayed and played there, forgetting our friend searching and guarding the tin until his mother called him in or darkness fell and he wandered away wondering at the silence of the street.

Follow-my-leader depended on the ability of the leader, usually Freddie, to devise ingenious and diverting routes and obstacles in our path. We followed him in strict order of precedence in the gang, my place usually being third or fourth, for though I lacked the animal daring of the others I made up for this in my powers of calculation concerning the best (for me) means of negotiating any obstacle. I was also a senior member of the gang so it was not fitting that I should be too far behind the leader. I also usually had persistence, and endured to the end of the route — though my performance on individual obstacles varied. I didn't mind falling in the brook, getting my feet wet or risking dangers that did not involve the hazard of falling from heights.

We usually began by jumping across the brook, and the less agile of us landed nearer the water than the dry safety of the other side. We then had to scamper up the sheer and slippery grassy bank to the railway line, given a limited number of strides. The next, and trickier dare, was to walk several hundred yards along the railway line and past the signal box without being seen and shouted at by the signalman. The passing of a train, and the consequent dive back down the bank for cover added to the excitement! Following this mission, we usually decided to walk along the narrow iron supports of the railway bridge: if we missed a support with both hand and foot we fell in the river. Happily this seldom happened, for it was a long drop. The final dare was to climb over the wire fence into Granny Clark's backyard and quickly onto the roof of her chicken shed — without disturbing the chickens. Granny Clark enjoyed this as much as we did, for she soon sensed the gang's arrival, and would stand behind the curtain of her bedroom window, which overlooked the chicken shed, armed with a saucepan of cold water which, at the decisive moment in his uneasy tenancy of the rickety roof of the shed, she would hurl over the unfortunate contestant. After the third or fourth contestant the chickens, too, set up an almost continual squawk of excitement; and we had to time our ascent to the roof to concur with one of Granny Clark's expeditions downstairs to fill her two saucepans with water. Another useful ploy was to have one of the gang knock on her door when one of us was ready to negotiate the shed roof. But unless he were careful and swift of foot the knocker at the door might also be greeted with a panful of water, while Granny's eyes gleamed.

If on one of our expeditions to the refuse bank, we found an old pram, then we made a gambo. This consisted of fitting a wooden base, usually an old box, onto the wheels of the pram, and then riding it down convenient hills or sloping streets. When the gang managed to make three or four gambos there were diverting gambo races, usually culminating in races down the severely sloping but greasy mountainside. This would continue for weeks until one of the gang had a more or less serious accident, breaking a leg or arm; after which event the gambos, on pain of punishment at home, were left neglected in the backyard, or given to the girls as prams.

The girls, who didn't of course belong to the gang, usually played hopscotch on the pavement, chalking their patchwork squares. It was a game we despised, and the boys sometimes amused themselves by peeing over the carefully drawn lines when the girls and any grown-ups living nearby were out of sight. The other great delight of the girls was swinging around the lamp-post, and often in the late evenings, when it was too dark to play elsewhere in the neighbourhood, we all gathered round the light of the street lamp, the boys cadging or bullying a go on the swings.

In a sentimental mood we would even join the girls in singing our songs and rhymes around the pools of light.

It was the girls' delight to play at 'houses' on the other side of the riverbank. They would bring their dolls and bits and pieces of discarded furniture, scrounged articles of clothing for dressing-up; and on long summer evenings they would build up quite a cosy 'house' in one of the dingles. We sometimes joined them, but soon usually ended up wrecking their cherished articles of furniture, and tearing their dressing-up clothes in our fights. These games of 'house' in the dingle came to an abrupt end for me on my return from a brief stay in hospital. I had, at a relatively late age, been circumcised. Clearly the inquisitive girls had heard some version of this matter, and on one occasion, when I was the only boy playing with them, they undressed me for inspection. I cannot recall that I resisted, or was embarrassed, but I was ordered not to play with them again.

It was the arrival of Tony which really stimulated sexual awareness among the boys. Tony was one of the evacuees from London, in our class in school. He sat at the back of the class, and it was his habit, when he decided the lesson was boring, to open his flies, grin and whisper to the nearby boys 'look at my prick', which he proudly displayed, slightly levering himself up, on the lid of his desk. Fortunately, our teacher, Mr Hopkin Bream, known as 'Fish', was short-sighted, elderly, and seldom needed to leave the island of his desk at the front of the classroom, spending the morning glancing at his newspaper there, and in the afternoon occasionally yawning, startled to attention only when a fly entered his open mouth — an event we speculated on and waited for with more delight than Tony's display.

Once his mouth snapped shut in anger and embarrassment when, teaching the correct usage of 'to, too, and two' Tony uncharacteristically raised his hand to volunteer an answer and Fish signalling him to speak and smiling at this unusual contributor, Tony with straight face and expressionlessly replied 'I have lost my two balls'. But Mr Hopkin Bream's ignorance of the back row exhibition remained, since no one else chose to copy the act in the publicity of the classroom.

The interlude with the girls on the grassy bank resulted in one of my periodic withdrawals from the company of the street, this time through maternal compulsion rather than personal choice. It was summer, so I decided to take up gardening, quickly purchasing a toy wheelbarrow and a rake; for in winter we used the garden as a convenient rubbish dump and there was the year's supply of empty tin cans, used small coal, the customary variety of household rubbish, and the stones that uncultivated gardens successfully accumulate, to be transported to the river bank.

It took me a week to shift the rubbish, and arrange the garden into a series of flower beds, their boundaries shaped by rough stones. I had also that week been studying the colourful flower seed packets in the corner shop window, deciding to plant Sweet William, Marigolds and Lupin; and so I invested in a packet of each, very taken with the vivid colour-illustrations. After some hours' close analysis of the illustrated flowers it seemed to me that, as they were to grow to a height of between one and two feet, they would need a pretty firm foundation in order to support their tall slender stems of bright blooms. So I proceeded to dig a two feet deep trench around the garden, acquiring many new piles of stones in the process. The trench completed, I carefully deposited the seeds in it, each one six inches from the other and two feet deep. With a sense of achievement I filled in the trench, carting extra earth from the river bank.

Every day for three months I watered and weeded my flower trench, growing disconsolate and an ill-humoured gardener, loudly complaining to my grandmother at the flowers' stubborn refusal to appear. Annoyance gave way to temper, temper to tears of frustration. My grandmother explained the folly of my planting the seeds too deep in the ground, and comfortingly confirmed that they would bloom in Australia. I got out my Atlas and it seemed indeed so, and in accord with the same logic by which I had reasoned the two foot foundation in earth was necessary to sustain their slender stems. I wrote several letters of inquiry to Australia, but they remained unanswered.

I joined the gang for an expedition 'up the monkey', the remotest part of the valley where the pit was on the roadside, miners' terraced houses spreading out from it like a spider's web. The boys there were tougher, fiercer, yet called you 'wus' with savage friendliness. It was popularly known as 'the monkey' seemingly since the practice of attaching gunpowder for underground explosives to such agile, fearless, hungry boys at the turn of the century. The boys would crawl monkey-like carrying their deadly burden along the cramped underground gullies and low tunnels. Powder-monkeys their name then, they still had skills of lithe daring and guile. We always travelled Indian file 'up the monkey', for it was exciting enemy territory, and a gaunt fortress-like citadel heralded 'the monkey', a lodging-house for nomadic miners as well as a vast wild-West pit-head pub.

But summer brought two historic incidents in the life of the street, our neighbour Sophia's car and next door's removal.

Friends and Neighbours

Our relations with our neighbours, due partly to my grandmother's sense of detachment and a distaste for too close involvement with the life of the street, were always tentative and spasmodic. We joined its community life only on particular and special occasions, such as the 'Victory' street teas in 1945. Even at such events as the arrival of Sophia's car or a next-door family removal by horse and cart, we preferred the role of sympathetic spectators.

It was one hot summer's afternoon that Sophia, with self-conscious pleasure, came across to speak to us, standing on the doorstep in the early afternoon sun. She was unusually pleased and rubbed her fat untidy hands against her plump freckled face, nervously bursting with the news she was plucking up courage to tell us. A lame old mongrel sniffed past. I patted the dog and they all looked to relieve the gossipy housewife tension.

'Did you enjoy yourselves last night?' asked Sophia.

'Very nice', replied my grandmother. '"The Lamb's" dart team won, so there was plenty to drink all round. Why didn't you come up?'

Sophia paused, visibly moved at the thought of the evening's entertainment, a tear of disappointment trickling self-consciously down her now half-joyous, half-sad flabby face. Wildly flapping her hands about her cheek to brush it away, like an over-coy concert-party soprano, she shuffled up to the doorstep and blurted out quickly: 'Well, Dai's been saving'. She laughed nervously and seizing courage said 'We got about £30'.

She beamed shyly like a goose who has laid a golden egg, and surveyed the hot summer-smelling street like an expansive millionaire. Then, gasping for breath in her excitement, her sweating face glistening in the heat of the sun and the heat of the moment, exploding with pent-up emotion, for all the world like

52

a giant stick of dynamite, Sophia gingerly drew closer and in a voice reduced to a whisper by emotion: 'Dai wants to buy a car!' It was out. So that's why they'd not been up 'The Lamb' since Easter.

Sophia was now blushing profusely, going from red to white like a setting sun with hiccoughs; she rubbed her large hands even more feverishly about her apple-dumpling face. The mongrel sat down, stock-still on the pavement as though conscious of the dramatic events taking place. We pocketed our half-mocking smiles in sympathy and chattered on as nonchalantly as we could; longing all the time to run in and savour the news all to ourselves. I pulled my grandmother's apron, already bored — 'Gran, can I come up "The Lamb" tonight?' The confession made, Sophia decided to waddle back across the street. Dai wanted his tea; we could see him, peering at us with his one eye, from the window of the house opposite, fascinated and fidgeting like inquisitive boys at a seaside peep-show. Dai, very precise, liked his tea on time.

Sophia turned to go, we waved and shouted goodbye. She crossed the road with a new dignity befitting the solemnity of the information she had just made known, her sweating hands covering the hole in her apron, and she entered into the house opposite, pleased as a battleship that in the pride of old age has sunk a rowing boat in home waters. The mongrel followed her in procession.

Next morning the noise of hammering, the scurrying of people at such an early hour woke me in my small front bedroom. I stared, dozily, out of the window and rubbed my eyes in amazement, not sure whether I was still dreaming. The hammering and excitement, which seemed soaring to a crescendo, centred round some margarine boxes, old posts and rusty tin sheets: a ramshackle shed was in the process of erection. The gurgling chuckle of Sophia as she surveyed the growing edifice brought me to my senses — it was a garage they were building. I ran to my grandmother's bedroom at the back of the house, excitedly jumping onto the bed whose ornamental brass shone in the clear morning sunlight. 'Come quick, Gran, come and see Sophia's garage! They're building it now.' Reluctantly, but otherwise unable to quench my excitement, my Grandmother followed me to my bedroom.

Dai, his one eye glaring with concentration, fixing now on one, now on another centre of activity, darting about like a jackie-jumper, was conducting operations.

'Gi's a shove yer!'

'Let's have a couple of nails, Jim. — Blast that sledge!'

'Daro, she's coming on lovely, fair play for everybody too, it'll be a nice shed when it's finished — you watch.'

'Garage,' snapped Dai quickly.

His sons slaved with pleasure on their pyramid. Children on their way to school loitered and gazed in awe. Sophia, her hands on her belly, apron fluttering in the morning breeze, smiled indulgently on all and sundry; she stood motionless in her complete contentment. She patted the mongrel, unable to contain her joy.

No more was heard or seen for a few weeks. The garage, like a pile of over-grown match boxes with margarine labels on, gradually became a part of the street; by day, being the street's latest novelty, it became the meeting place of the gang, and at school we bragged and fabled it held a spaceship ready to leap to the witching moon.

Sophia did not come across to gossip with us in all this time; no doubt too conscious of the attendant fruits of their labour to be seen abroad before fulfilment. As if to remedy the shame of an empty garage the mongrel had pups in the shed.

The street grew weary and disappointed, friends lost interest and neighbours grew critical. 'Having a car!' declared my father, 'they couldn't afford a scooter!'

'And as for that dog's kennel!' chorused the neighbours. It echoed from door to door.

Tick-tock, tick-tock, tick-tock, our grandfather clock ticked time happily away in the kitchen. And on the Saturday of August bank holiday everything was especially clean and shining for the occasion, and the brasses above the fireplace gleamed in the sunlight that streamed through the window. They had been rubbed and polished the night before and now they were yellow and golden as the sun itself. A fire burned half-heartedly in the grate, almost put out by the sun's rays. But even the fire was burning tidily, not roaring all over the grate as it usually did and spitting small coal about the place. The table was laid for dinner, and even the cushions on the chairs kept their places carefully. The cat, sleeping on the couch, had given himself a thorough wash, so that his white fur looked white and the black looked black, not just dirty. He snoozed, both eyes shut — which was unusually lax for him and sure guarantee no storms were ahead, meteorological or emotional.

Ianto, lodging then next door, looked around uneasily as he came in the back way. In his dreams the cat winced and opened one eye. Realising how quiet it was Ianto shouted:

'Hello! Anybody in? It's me. Come to see if you want a raffle ticket.' Hearing no reply he stared around the kitchen as though he had inadvertently overlooked its occupants, then convinced it was empty he walked to the front door.

'Oh, there you are', he beamed, seeing us standing on the doorstep. 'Well, Ianto, what do you think of the car?' said my grandmother. 'What car?' inquired Ianto, staring in short-sighted wonder as though he ought to see a lion squatting on the pavement before him, so he took off his glasses to see better.

'It's the car. It's come!' said my grandmother with finality. 'They're just going to ride in it now. Stand there to watch and be quiet!' We made room for Ianto on the step, which already held my mother, my grandmother and myself. All along the street groups were gathered at their front doors, each household accommodating relations and friends. The news had spread, like tidings of a funeral or a wedding.

Sophia came first out of the house: all fifteen stone decorously fitted in a new black dress for the occasion. Blushing coyly, a young bride again, she smiled at the assembled neighbours, nervous and proud. Behind her came Dai, also in new black, a flower in his buttonhole. He smiled, severely, and against the grain. With the calculated ceremony of a dowager Sophia stepped aside while he opened the car door. She stepped forward, easing herself into the back seat of the old Ford, issuing smiles and blushes like a fountain water. All the gang had assembled on the nearby pavement to cheer and jeer, but in some awe. I stood distantly on the doorstep. Dai sat, precisely, beside Sophia. Her sons got in the front — Bill was driving.

'How about one for the road, Sophia love?' shouted Aunty Martha, rushing out with a glass of beer from 'The Lamb'. Seeing Sophia already settled in the car, Martha stood on the pavement to drink the beer, smiling and waving at the car.

On the doorstep outside Sophia's house the mongrel whined, tears in her old, loving eyes, thinking it was a funeral.

'Oh, love her! Come on in Daisy! In the car with Mam. Let her come, Bill.' The dog, without second bidding, leaped through the open window into the car, full of doggy affection, and began licking Sophia's face like a barmaid wiping a beer counter, all wet and with gusto.

'Sit down, Daisy fach. Sit down, love,' coaxed Sophia, a little perplexed now. And at last Daisy settled, contentedly, on her widespread lap.

The car set off. 'An epic moment,' muttered my grandmother. The gang cheered and whistled, and the neighbours smiled and waved. Slowly up the street it moved with all the dignity of a hearse. The assembled neighbours smiled and chatted their pleasure, and Sophia acknowledged her audience with a regal wave of the hand. Daisy barked with ceremonial regularity, like an execution drum roll.

'Beautiful! Lovely! If only my Auntie Sarah was alive to see it,' exclaimed Ianto.

'Don't be sentimental, Ianto,' snapped my grandmother. 'Sarah even thought oil lamps the work of the devil. If she hadn't refused to use anything but candles she wouldn't have burned to death!' Ianto shuffled uneasily on the step at the reprimand.

'Jezebel that she is, riding up the street in that car with no shame at all of it,' shouted Mrs Bowen the Apostolic who lived a few doors above us and no longer addressed us directly, remembering and fearing my grandmother's scalding and contemptuous dismissal 'You'd hold a candle for the devil for a ha'penny!'

'Oh, fair play now, Mrs Bowen fach. It's different from when we....'

A sudden bang and clatter of brakes brought swift and complete silence. At the top of the road stood the car, not moving an inch. They pushed and shoved and they swore and they kicked, but it would not budge. Everyone stared, horrified, not speaking, as though the end of the world had come there in the middle of the street. Sophia emerged, drooping like a lily the week after Palm Sunday. With tears in her eyes she walked quietly, her head bowed, down the street.

'Oh, love her! What a shame!'

'Never mind, Sophia. The car'll be all right tomorrow — I'm sure, love!' condoled the neighbours, enjoying now the tragedy as they had earlier the comedy.

'A judgment it is! A judgment,' exulted Mrs Bowen.

In silence Sophia walked into the house, Cassandra-like with gloom. Her sons, in disgust, pushed the car into the gutter and retired to 'The Lamb' opposite to drown their sorrows. A bedraggled Daisy followed Sophia, her tail between her legs.

'I'll never be able to hold my head up again. Shamed me you have! Shamed me!' wailed Sophia. 'Remember, Dai, it's a horse-drawn carriage — with plumes — will carry my coffin after this. You can keep them old cars.'

The street returned to its business, so we went into the spick-and-span kitchen to buy our raffle tickets. Ianto bobbed about with glee at his forthcoming sale, like an over-wound robot.

'First prize a car,' he said, smiling to himself, 'one for the road!' But soon Ianto took to the road himself, though only to the next street.

The Removal

All was quiet for a few weeks until the removal of Ianto and Polly, my uncle and aunt, to the distant and different life of the next street. A few days before, Ianto came in excitedly to tell us they had hired Caradoc and his horse and cart to transport them. 'He's only charging 8/6d,' explained Polly shyly when we chatted to her on the doorstep.

When the morning of the departure had arrived even my grandmother was up for breakfast, and the sun shone loudly down the street. By half past nine they were ready to begin next door, and Ianto hit on the wall with a hammer to let us know.

'Can I come in with you, Gran?' I appealed, unable to contain my excitement. To have been refused this adventure would have been the worst death in the world.

'Yes, but keep quiet till I'm ready.' With dismay, I saw my grandmother place her curling tongs in the fire. It would take nearly an hour for her to be ready now that she was going to curl her hair and change her clothes.

'Make a list of the furniture on your blackboard,' said my grandmother. I put up my board and easel and miserably began listing next door's furniture from memory as well as dashing out to inspect the slowly accumulating items on the pavement.

'How do you spell couch, Gran?'

'C-o-u-c-h,' my grandmother patiently and carefully spelled out my queries while she curled her hair. Soon waiting became a pleasure.

'Do the kitchen things first,' commanded my grandmother, her pedagogic instinct for classification and order uppermost. 'Then the middle room, and then the parlour.'

'How do you spell shepherd?' I had reached the religious pictures that hung in the parlour.

'Fetch my black dress from the wardrobe upstairs first and the silver brooch I had from Aunty Delia last Christmas.' I scurried upstairs as my grandmother shouted after me, 'it's in the Coronation Jug on the dressing table.'

Dressed as on a special occasion up 'The Lamb', in a severe black brightened only by the silver brooch, my grandmother was at last ready. I had filled both sides of the blackboard.

In next door's kitchen Ianto, dapper as a sandboy, fussed; fidgeted; walked from room to room; did nothing; got in the way; fell over his feet; got nowhere fast. By the time we'd arrived he was a nervous wreck.

'Come on, Polly! The cart'll be here soon. It will probably rain, and we haven't moved half the stuff yet.'

Polly, his wife, sat primly, still finishing her late breakfast and joined now by my grandmother over another cup of tea. She refused to get worked up. She had moved house before. She knew all about it. And she was not a child.

'Sit down, Ianto. There's plenty of time. Sit down quiet before I throw something at you!' snapped Polly.

Ianto left the room; came back; lost his glasses; sat on them; couldn't find them; hunted through his pockets; went into all the other rooms to look for them; returned.

'Polly, where's my glasses? Can't find them anywhere! Have you seen them?'

'What do you think I want them for? Haven't I got glasses of my own?' replied Polly coldly.

Seeing them on the chair Ianto smiled to himself at his find. He put them on excitedly, as though for the first time.

'Go and help Ianto carry more furniture out. You can get most of it down between you,' directed my grandmother, irritated by the scene.

'I'll take the best parlour pictures then, shall I,' smiled Ianto, nervously, in question, fearing my grandmother's as well as Polly's sharp tongue now. Whenever he moved he carried these two pictures first into the new house, proudly, excitedly, yet coyly, like a new bride. The large gleaming bright and silvery paintings on glass of two monstrous peacocks, each glaring at the other as though about to do battle, were treasured family heirlooms. In the early morning sunlight they gleamed even more ferociously: hostile household gods.

The furniture was piling up on the pavement: pictures, tables, boxes of china and linen, fire-irons, beds, chairs, two couches, a china plaque of Lord Kitchener and a striking painting on glass of Christ admonishing the woman taken in sin. It was a glorious summer's morning: comfortable for doing nothing, but soon bringing sweat and curses to amateur furniture removers. Forewarned, and seeing overtures in the display of goods on the pavement, the other neighbours of the street began assembling. The more determinedly curious placed armchairs outside their doorways, intent on enjoying themselves in comfort; put the kettle on the fire; and sat, and waited. The little groups got bigger as the minutes ticked by. The children, of course, felt compelled to play their games on this day outside our house, though at reverential distance from the assembled wares. Even the gang slouched, joked and held mock fights nearby. The house and its departing inhabitants were today apart from the rest of the street; as in a wedding or a funeral familiar relationships were disbanded, and the departing couple were worthy of the respect paid to the dead or the about to be wed.

The furniture successfully hauled onto the pavement, Ianto returned to the kitchen to inform Polly and my grandmother, who were now sentimental over flagons of beer.

Towards dinner time the heavy summer heat began to stifle. Still the horse and cart did not come. Now only occasional figures were seated at the doorways, often a grandfather with nothing else to do, ready to signal the others should events begin. The odd pieces of furniture, the banked up linen, the elaborate china ornaments, trying not to look obtrusive, seemed to grow out from the wall of the house. My grandmother had sent me to guard the furniture and stacked possessions in between expeditions up 'The Lamb' to re-fill the flagon. But by now I was getting over-excited.

The gossips chatted, neighbours beamed their goodwill, nodding in my direction as they spoke, yet viewing the household goods almost coyly, as though they oughtn't to, or it didn't belong.

'We're praying for rain,' mocked one of the gang, assuming attitudes of oriental prayer.

The town clock struck twelve. And on the last stroke, by

accident or design, Caradoc, his horse, his cart and his sheep dog turned the corner of the street. Immediately an excited murmur went from door to door; the street regained its onlookers as though by magic, and Caradoc, sitting in regal state on the cart, moved in procession down the centre of the street. He was an odd and very old wizened man, but, especially, he was odd, an ancient, Celtic satyr who sang imprecisely obscene songs in Welsh to his horse as they ambled along and who, he claimed, didn't understand 'the English'.

The first cart-load was ready. Caradoc, now sad and solemn as undertaker and hearse, walked alongside the horse. His sheep dog barked at his heels in encouragement, a fiery excitable beast. I walked with Ianto behind the cart lest anything should fall off, and the procession set off to the obvious satisfaction of all and sundry. Slowly, with dignity, we moved up the street: the occasion too solemn for banter from the assembled neighbours. I pushed back a large spotted china dog eager to fall off the overfull cart. Caradoc, guiding the horse, was singing in Welsh; and to the unfamiliar tune Taliesin ambled, an old creature and obviously sentimental at heart. The song rang in my ears; the sweat poured from me; the sheep dog yelped at ten second intervals; the odd shapes of furniture became hazy. It was like a strange, inexplicable, childhood dream.

At the top of the street, opposite 'The Lamb', stood the corner shop. As we came round its customers waved to us from the windows and opened doorway.

'Where you going? Camping is it?' yelled a fat, heavy-breasted woman, and fell helpless with laughter onto a sack of potatoes, so that you couldn't tell where she finished and the sack began.

Arriving at the new house, the horse was stopped, the sheep dog ceased his processional bark; we unloaded. Then back, and another load. Seeing us turn the corner, the children cheered in pent-up anticipation, and the gang whistled and jeered. I sat with Ianto on the cart, now empty on its return, smug as heroes come back from Troy. We knew. We had moved the furniture, and were about to do so again — you watch.

The third load, the fourth — Taliesin was an old horse and could not carry much. With successive journeys the dignity of our trafficking had worn off, the novelty had gone and the banter came fast and free. Since the second journey Caradoc and Ianto had stopped at each passing for a pint, and my grandmother's salon was now in full afternoon session. At each halt Titus stood ready at the door, two pints in hand: soothing Welsh bitter in the hot afternoon sunshine. Today the gossips grinned their approval. The mood was Rabelaisian. Mrs Davies the Pavement, so named because of the stone flags that fronted her house and that she scrubbed morning and evening, put out her two deckchairs. Radiant with her domestic vigour and beaming with satisfaction after a busy morning cleaning house and pavement, she took off her apron and sat in one of the chairs. Looking up and down the street at the gossiping neighbours she triumphantly declared 'I could have knocked doors out of windows this morning!'

Only the dressing table now remained, waiting in state on the pavement. It sprawled, massive and angular: a series of drawers, carved knobs, gargoyle-like embellishments and a whole riff-raff of grandiose effects. A piece of Victorian beauty. It was so angular, so consistently shapeless that, had it been a diva, it would have been corseted beyond recognition. Being in its natural, uninhibited, armophous state it sprawled. But at last it was on the cart. We left on the last trip. There was a time for tears, and the sylphs wept. The putti pouted.

The door of the new house was small. The windows smaller. Even should it go through the door, the dressing table could not wind its way up the stairs, a narrow jutting determined stone spiral.

'Damn and blast! Damn and blast!' shouted Ianto. 'It'll 'ave to go through the bedroom window.'

The sheep dog, at the news, barked even more excitedly. The words of Caradoc's song sounded even more Welsh and curiously obscene, as he envisaged the contortions that would be necessary. The neighbours broke into smiles, and chattered wildly at this quite unexpected *deus ex machina*.

'And how are we, then, going to get the dressing table up to the window?' asked Caradoc, so amazed that he uttered the question slowly, syllable by syllable, with slow speculation. We sat in the gutter to discuss tactics, Ianto and Caradoc lit cigarettes, and I was sent to 'The Lamb' for two pints of bitter.

The arrival of Polly broke up our councils.

'Quick, boys, let's have the kitchen table out on the pavement. Under the bedroom window by there. Careful now! Gentle with 'er boys!' — directed Ianto who, straightaway, skipped upstairs to receive the dressing table as it came towards the window, swaying like a farouche dinosaur.

'Careful now boys. Gentle with 'er. Ease her off your shoulders ... Watch you won't fall off the kitchen table! — Blast! Damn and blast! It's stuck! Won't budge an inch! Shove hard boys! Shove like hell!'

The men assisting shoved, but to no avail. The dressing table, jammed securely, swayed half in, half out of the window. I gazed in awe and fascination as it hovered four feet above my head.

'Keep 'er steady with the brush, boys, while Caradoc fetches a saw. I'll watch she don't fall back' — yelled Ianto frantically from above, clinging to the other end of the dressing table like a lover. Valiantly I held the sweeping brush aloft, its head only just tickling the dressing table. Already my arm ached with the effort, the dressing table inches beyond my firm reach. But the sky had darkened. It started to rain. I put on my new, shiny red sou'wester. It was a Christmas present I was keeping for New Year's Eve, our great festive, holy night of the year.

Years Old and New

It was on New Year's Eve that our house was thrown open to all the friends and neighbours who belonged to my grandmother's drinking fraternity, of whom the 'kitchen friends' formed the nucleus. And the last day of December still burns brightly in memory, however desolate the dying year, the ashes of childhood still glowing in the grate.

The log, specially selected and prepared for the occasion, was noisily burning away the old year, sending sparks and long glancing yellow flames high up the chimney. All were locked in 'Auld Lang Syne', and on the wireless Big Ben slowly chimed midnight:

'Happy New Year, love.'

'Happy New Year, Gran.'

'Happy New Year, Florrie.'

'Happy New Year, Martha.'

It was in: a year of departures and change.

'Wonder what kind of year it'll be for us?' mused my grandmother.

'Come on now, folks, let's finish the kissing', chirped Ianto. Ianto was doggo. And sentimental to the marrow.

'Together, everybody, let's sing "The log was burning brightly",' ordered my grandmother.

Aunty Martha began sweeping away the old year, out through the backdoor, brandishing the brush with deft movements, though far gone after six hours of drinking.

'Sweep the old year out I will if it's the last thing I do. Always have done it. Always will. Till I go to the grave. And two shillings for the first dark haired young man who knocks. Always have been. Always will. Till I go to the grave.' Aunty Martha made her annual New Year speech.

'You've swept all the old year out now, Martha,' said my grandmother. 'Come and join the circle.'

Garth Colliery, c.1903, and the memorial illustration from the *Glamorgan Gazette* for the nine men and boys who died at the colliery in the disaster in 1897. Among those killed was Tom Ackerman's fifteen year old brother George.

Clockwise, my sister Barbara riding her tricycle in Cwmdu Street with a friend; nursing the cat with a friend, on my gardening plot facing next door's chicken shed; pushing my cousin in the pram; clearing snow in Cwmdu Street, aged four.

Clockwise. Nursed by my mother; on an outing to the Forest of Dean from 'The Lamb', from the right my uncle who held the record in mining most coal in a day during the war, next his wife, then my fortune-telling aunt, a cousin-in-law; my grandmother on the Forest of Dean trip.

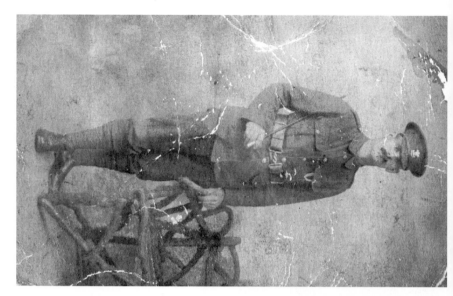

Tom Ackerman, died in action, February 1917; documents concerning his death, his burial at Bray, and late payment of war pension arrears. The letter awarding Jack McCarthy the Military Medal for helping men escape from burning tanks.

My mother with her sister, who went to London in service, photographed near Cwmdu Street and at the local photographic studio.

'The Lamb' inside and out. *Above*, friends and family celebrating at 'The Lamb', my mother and two aunts seated in the corner. *Below*, 'The Lamb' today, sadly defunct, with Cwmdu Street to the right, the railway line, embankment and bridge at the end.

Above, the family grave in Llangynwyd Churchyard, near Maesteg*Below*, the wedding of my aunt in service in London. Rear: my grandmother, grandfather and fortune-telling aunt; my mother is front left.

Above, view towards the railway line and bridge, with the backs of Cwmdu Street houses, the river and allotments. *Below*, view from the other side of the railway line, river and bridge; in the distance the school, valley and mountains beyond.

'Must sweep the old year out before letting in the new,' contin-
ued Martha, 'there'll be no luck otherwise, mixing the old with
the new.' And Martha flourished the broom stick like a Trojan.
A dark young man arrived by arrangement, and Martha con-
cluded her rites.

We knew my grandmother was about to recite, and all enjoyed
the suspense of the silence as she moved with stern, dramatic
purpose to her place before the crackling logs on the fire. As in a
theatre at the rise of the curtain the room was quick with antici-
pation, suppressed excitement, all eyes were fixed on her rapt,
unseeing, compelling gaze upon us. The sparks and flames from
the burning logs abetted the drama of her opening stillness and
silence. Then she raised her arms in command:

> Ring out, wild bells, to the wild sky,
>> The flying cloud, the frosty light:
>> The year is dying in the night,
> Ring out, wild bells, and let him die.

Pausing she surveyed the room, resuming in full thespian vein,
now with subdued joy, now in clarion tones:

> Ring out the old, ring in the new,
>> Ring, happy bells, across the snow:
>> The year is going, let him go;
> Ring out the false, ring in the true.

Her socialism burned with the passion and anger of age as she
gave contemporary urgency to Tennyson's lires:

> Ring out the feud of rich and poor,
> Ring in redress to all mankind....
>> Ring out the want, the care, the sin,
> The faithless coldness of the times....
>> Ring out the narrowing lust of gold.

She finished in stage whisper as she called for 'The larger heart,
the kindlier hand'. Then requests came for favourite dramatic
monologues particularly 'Curfew Shall Not Ring Tonight', still
telling of the girl who clung to the bell to save her condemned
lover. It was succeeded by 'The Charge of the Light Brigade' and

after the exhortations of 'Half a league, half a league/ Half a league onward' the New Year was challengingly launched.

Soon the party resumed its convivial, drinkers' gusto. Frothing pints of beer were filled endlessly from the barrel under the stairs in the kitchen. Since one o'clock fearful rumours that it was about to go dry had been spreading, but always they proved false: the beer came, frothing and jovial. 'And in plenty — like water from a tap, only better,' declared Eddie, bald, squat, his eyes watering with pleasure, and bubbling with satisfaction as he ran the barrel. With each round of drinks he became even jollier than before, and mothered the barrel like a baby.

Going through the back kitchen on the way to the lavatory the ladies paid their respects to Eddie and the barrel. As the lavatory was outside the house, and some few yards' walk beyond the back door, the ladies preferred to tootle down just outside the back door. They made sorties in groups of two or three, and it was my job to stand in the kitchen, a sentry at the back door, to warn the men they must wait. This situation always produced much merriment, and I would long with mounting excitement for Evan the Milk to give his performance; though anticipated in the first hours of drinking, Evan the Milk always cannily waited till the ladies were oblivious and sufficiently befuddled with beer. Then, in a sequinned dress of pink silk, complete with blond wig and heavy make-up, Evan the Milk would suddenly appear at the back door, wink conspiratorially at me, and join the bevy of women already noisily and chattily tootling down. Soon screams of shocked merriment and delight would come from the backyard, Evan the Milk's parody grown bold and comic. At this point, swishing his skirts, rolling his eyes, and fingering his straw-coloured wig, dashes of lipstick smearing his lips, Evan the Milk would enter the room of the party in gay triumph. Privy to the plot, my grandmother would be waiting in the passageway, dressed in Jack's old army uniform, resplendent with first world war medals, Titus's best black funeral bowler hat, borrowed for the occasion, and brandishing a silver topped walking stick. Evan the Milk's prima donna swirl concluded, my grandmother would enter, severe and unsmiling, and to renewed applause did her song, mime, and dance with Evan the Milk, while Aunty Martha played the piano accompaniment of 'Where are you going to my pretty maid?'. 'Where are you going to, my pretty maid?' sang my grandmother, a stern, predatory toff, tipping her bowler and flourishing her silver stick. 'I'm going a-milking, Sir I say, Sir I say. I'm going a-milking, Sir I say' responded Evan the Milk, with coy but winking lasciviousness, raising his elaborate skirts a little and shaking his large white milking pail.

'What is your fortune, my pretty maid?' intoned my grand-mother, more judge than philanderer.

'My face is my fortune, Sir I say, Sir I say,' grimaced Evan and in tones and gestures of high farce, repeating with a clown's lechery and exaggeration 'My face is my fortune, Sir I say!'

All awaited with tense excitement the loved and familiar dramatic finale, my grandmother introducing it brusquely and severely with 'Then I can't marry you, my pretty maid' and sternly repeating 'Then I can't marry you, my pretty maid!', scowling magnificently through the whole audience, who uneasily prepared themselves for Evan's coup-de-grâce. He moved to the centre of the room, heaving his stuffed bosoms, shuffling his silk skirts, and announced in high-pitched indignant shrieks:

'But *nobody* asked you Sir I say, Sir I say!' He stomped the carpet with his high heels; 'Oh *nobody* asked you, Sir I say!' At this point he flung the noisy milk pail to the floor, and we'd all edge back in fearful delight at Evan the Milk's joyous coup-de-foudre.

Martha's style of rapid improvisation changed immediately to 'Knees up Mother Brown', in which we all joined, romping about the room with mounting crescendo. It was the climax of the night's entertainment, as we all scurried out to the kitchen, struggling under and out from the large oilclothed kitchen table, singing and calling 'Knees up, Mother Brown! Under the table you must go, eeie-eeie-eeie-ho!', all in choral pursuit of the ecstatic Evan, ducking and diving under all available hideouts!

There was never any drunkenness in my grandmother's parties, the slow but steady lapping of halves of bitter keeping harmony with time and tide as the festivities unwound. Never but once, when grandson Jim on army leave, who'd spent the evening drinking competitive pints with his butties on an on-the-town pub tour, arrived late. Summoned to her party by my grandmother he arrived in uniform and continued amiably and affably drinking until he fell into a heavy but still smiling sleep, a dreaming, harmless, drunken child in battledress. Enraged and embarrassed his mother beat him about the head and body with her fists, exclaiming 'Wake up, Jim! You drunken bugger!'. But Jim slept smiling on, even when she poured his unfinished pint over him, now a serenely blithe Bacchus dripping in his damp khaki.

'Let the poor boy sleep now!' commanded Florrie, unsmiling. 'I'll have a word with him tomorrow — before he leaves for his embarkation.'

Then the New Year festivities took a sad, serious turn as we all sat quietly together and sang folk-songs, the singing veined with nostalgia and lost love's remembrance. They were the old drinking songs, often the Irish ballads that Jack McCarthy knew by heart, whether of 'Molly Malone', in Dublin's fair city, 'The Wild Colonial Boy', or 'She walked through the fair'; some with choruses all could join in and all with sentiments that could be sentimentally shared. Polly's rendering of 'Danny Boy' brought us all to tears. Many of Jack's friends were Irishmen who had come to work in the pits, joining the mining communities of the valleys. Paddy's day was an important social event in my grandmother's calendar, always of course a pub drinker's festive day. In contrast St David's day belonged to school and chapel eisteddfods.

Then our singing together turned to Victorian ballads. Aunty Martha always began with 'A bird in a gilded cage', telling how a poor young girl married a jealous, rich, grasping old man, so that all hearts were touched when we learned how 'her beauty was sold for an old man's gold' and all joined in the finale 'she's a bird in a gilded cage!' Much loved was Ianto's rendering of 'Thora', especially as he addressed in ringing tones his dead lover 'Come, come, come to me Thora!' and with a sorrow only the darkest heart could fail to share confessed 'I lov'd you in life too little! I love you in death too well!' As the more serious mood deepened and turned to otherworldly yearning and comradely endeavour the lively and popular Sankey hymns, so good for communal singing, held sway. 'Telephone to Glory!' returned the lost to child's fable and faith.

'Will your anchor hold?' brought back rousing and challenging tidings of shared hope and 'Throw out the life-line!' provided an operatic clamour in its choruses in that room of past and present at the turn of the year:

Throw out the Life-Line across the dark wave!
Someone is drifting away!
Throw out the Life-Line across the dark wave!
Someone is sinking today!

Then, magically, came the children's rites that the adults performed with full ceremony and solemnity, only a few of the men a little self-conscious. Both young and old delighted to be children still, formed a large circle in the room, holding hands, the chairs pushed back against the wall, and began their ritual play. In hand-held circle we slowly moved around the room singing of the handsome prince who came riding by and of the princess who lived in 'her high tower! Her high tower!', carefully aspirating the 'h' in childlike delight. As prince I proudly rode outside and the princess demurely waited within the circle, following magical rites. Then in the always popular 'Sir Roger is dead and lies in his grave' we enacted ceremonies of love and loss, life and death that led finally to our miming of 'Wallflowers, wallflowers, growing up so high! We are little children and we must all die!', mimetically raising our arms for the growing flowers. The named exceptions enjoyed a brief respite from mortality when called within the ring, but never quite breaking the haunting spell of mutability this song and play cast, with its common currency of flowers and children. 'Fair Rosa was a lovely child' was another lyric of tristesse we sang and acted in our enchanted, New Year's Eve circle and true festival of remembrance for the dead, in the wine-dark hours of poetry and pantomime.

An interval now in the various party activities gave the women a chance to go out the back. They eschewed the tricky walk in the dark to the outside lavatory. With its wide wooden seat, commodious enough for three, a bundle of newspapers on one side, it was a not uncomfortable place; though you had to carry a bucket of water from the kitchen tap conveniently near the back door for the cistern was usually unreliable.

At nights you needed a glimmering candle or torch. Our cats, too, especially when the house was crowded, were apt to make their den there, cat-napping under the bench-like seat, for they could sidle through the small gap between the top of the pan and the wooden seat, safe in its cobwebbed, hidden recesses. Forgetting their presence, one might sometimes feel an exploratory furry paw, aggressive or friendly.

It was my father's habit, after a few drinks, to go straight to bed on such occasions, not caring for party festivities; and during a later sortie to the back kitchen, I heard the voices of the women who'd gone outside to the yard raised in excited consternation. I opened the back door to investigate.

'It's raining terrible,' lamented Jinny, wiping the water from her white straw hat.

'Well, I'm lovely and dry over here,' replied Martha, a few feet away in the backyard, patting her dry hair in confirmation. 'It must have been raining fast when you came out. It's stopped now though.'

'No it's not!' declared Jinny, more irritably now, 'I can feel the drops still falling on my hat.'

'It's stopped, I tell you,' Martha asserted again. 'Look! I'm as dry as the desert.'

'Well, it's still raining over here, whatever,' insisted Jinny sharply, who was squatting farther away from the back door than Martha, and directly below the bedroom window.

'Well, I'm still dry as the desert. Look!' claimed Martha proudly, a successful Canute, and patting her now dishevelled but dry strands of grey hair furiously.

'Well, it's pissing down over here,' shouted Jinny angrily. 'You come and change places with me — with your bloody desert!'

The two women changed places.

Drops of water now splashed on Martha.

'You're quite right, Jinny love. There must be a leaking shoot or something over here.'

My grandmother banged the kitchen window — 'Hurry up you two! Are you going to stay out there all night? Reuben is going to sing, Jinny.'

'The old bugger can wait till I've dried my hat!' replied Jinny, as she and Martha ambled in.

'You've got a leaking shoot out there,' she added. 'I'll send Reuben to mend it tomorrow.'

Standing on the back doorstep now, I heard a creaking noise from above and looked up to the bedroom window. Grinning down at me, my father was standing in his underpants and closing the half-opened bedroom window in the dark.

'That'll teach the silly buggers,' he said and laughed.

And the moon went back behind a cloud.

In the centre of the room stood Reuben, his gold earrings flashing as they caught the firelight; he was ready to sing 'You're going to leave the old home, Jim.' As long as I could remember he had sung 'You're going to leave the old home, Jim', and wore gleaming earrings. Over the years even the slowest and drunkest had learned to anticipate each intonation of his voice, and how he would forget the third line of the fifth verse. It was always the same line he forgot, Reuben was nothing if not consistent. Somehow it added to the pleasure of the song, giving the right dramatic touch, for as Reuben approached the fifth verse he got nervouser and nervouser, and Jinny muttered audibly between sups of beer 'The old sod's going to bugger it up again. The old sod's going to bugger it up again.'

And always, without fail, he did.

Preparing for his song, Reuben glared round the room, taking note of everyone who was missing. He took out his large red and white spotted handkerchief ready, for always, at the same point near the end of the song, he would be overcome by the words of parting and cry like a baby.

'Lovely, beautiful — if only his mother could see him now,' sighed Martha. His mother being dead over thirty years, the pathos of her remark went straight to Reuben's gentle heart. His eyes began to fill with tears. He was near the end of the song. He was leaving the old home —

Suddenly, a wail from the kitchen rent the air. Reuben stopped in mid-note, his handkerchief held aloft, an aged Cupid. White in the face, Elektra-like, Eddie stepped solemnly into the room:

'The barrel's gone dry.'

Eddie uttered the words hoarsely, with difficulty, as though

71

speaking through gauze, like the ghost in Hamlet. Seldom were words more dramatic, more devastating. No-one spoke, only stared vacantly.

'It's two in the morning,' added Eddie disconsolately. 'Everywhere will be shut now.'

My grandmother walked to the centre of the room. 'Martha and I will go up "The Lamb" for another barrel,' she announced. 'They've got plenty in the cellar — it's there for drinking. We'll knock them up.' My grandmother put on her coat and hat and fox fur, and set off, striding out like a general to the field. Aunty Martha followed her.

The two women swayed arm in arm up the street, holding a candle which they guarded against going out as it rocked to and fro in their hands like a drunken glow-worm. It stood in the heavy brass candlestick. The town clock struck three a.m. A sheep bleated on the nearby hillside. Then, without warning, the women stopped; chatted a few seconds —

'I haven't got my hat, Florrie. Can't go without my hat — it's not respectable!' exclaimed Martha.

'Never mind. There's nobody to notice,' said my grandmother firmly.

After a second's hesitation, Martha continued forward. 'But it's not respectable!' she repeated.

They reached the pub. It was in complete darkness. My grandmother picked up some small stones and hurled them at the bedroom window. Martha held up the candle to give light.

'Titus! Titus! Get up! We want another barrel!'

A light went on in the room above. Titus, clad in a nightshirt, appeared at the window. He stared out, dazed and apprehensive.

'Go home now, girls — it's nearly four. Come back tomorrow, tidy.' A new shower of gravel hit the window.

'Get up and fetch us some beer before I come up there,' threatened Martha.

'All right, girls, all right,' said Titus quickly, now trembling at the window as a large stone whistled past his head.

'I'll be down now.'

The two women sat down on the pavement, exhausted after their endeavour, and I sat beside them. A bedraggled mongrel came up to investigate, licking our faces, pleased to find company in the cold, deserted night.

'Go away! Go away!' growled Martha, pushing the dog off. Titus appeared in the doorway.

He tried to lever the barrel onto a truck. But it was of no avail. He could not manipulate it alone in the dark, and it slipped from his grasp. Sliding off the truck it began to roll down the street. Breaking the dead silence of night, it rolled on down the street, thundering as it gathered speed like the last call to Judgment in the hollow and muffled night. It raced past our house and on towards the river bank. From the house came sounds of continued merriment, as the festivities got new energy with the approach of morning. 'Roll out the barrel', sang the second group setting off for more drink; this time in earnest. A new dawn crept unwillingly into the sky, while in the other houses the lights were switched on as some got ready for the morning shift.

'We'll manage it this time,' declared my grandmother firmly. 'These men can help Titus with the loading. It's only a matter of transport! The others will search the river-bank!

'Here, you take this!' she commanded me, handing over the brass candlestick.

Leading the procession, a bacchanalian choirboy, I carried the candle, pale postulant in the dawn-streaked dark.

Willingly to School

Our local school was within five minutes of home, but through-out childhood the journey there, via the excitements of the river bank, and the length of the adjoining street with a brief slanging match, if not a pitched battle with a rival gang, usually involved a half hour's adventures; so we were always late. It was a pleasant school, built by a progressive local authority. But as our neighbourhood was at the opposite end from the 'posh' part of the town, and the pupils in attendance mostly the children of miners and the unemployed, the teachers were freer to pass the time as pleasantly as possible, less impeded by dry academic endeavour. Seldom did anyone from our area pass the scholarship examination for entry to the local Grammar School; and in consequence, and very sensibly, there was little emphasis on cramming and routine instruction for this examination. Few had any scholastic ambition, or did any homework.

My own arrival at the Infants Department had been far from propitious. I was first taken to school as a four-year-old early starter. I had already learned, from my grandmother's tutelage, to write my name and address on my board and easel. My insistence on adding to the address 'in my granny's house', however, was a gratuitous precision in information that was not much appreciated by my class mates. I was also able to read, and not impressed by the toys and coloured blocks offered me for my instruction and amusement. However, I adored the doll's house. And the trouble occurred at the end of school that first day when I kicked and screamed and howled, in my spoilt way, because I was compelled to leave without it. Having had little contact with other children, and brought up exclusively with adult compan-ions, my rage did not easily subside.

There was a note to my parents suggesting I was not yet ready for school, and so was left another year at home, with the board

74

and easel and reading-books of my grandmother's daily tutelage, the doll's house a memory. I patiently awaited my fifth birthday and returned. The scene repeated itself over possession of the Noah's Ark, for that nautical and esoteric home with its varied and delightful inhabitants gave such joy! But this time I stayed at school, though that Christmas I tramped the war-time Cardiff stores with my mother in vain search for a toyshop ark.

But school, for the most part, made curiously little impact on us, and interfered very little with our education, as we derived our deepest and most awakening experiences from the life of the neighbourhood, whether the crowded vitality of the street, or roving the surrounding hillsides. At school, it was playtime and dinner hour which were most significant, where our games and fights and rivalries held sway. I can remember only one fight, for I was sufficiently wary not to get involved with fights since most of the boys were tougher and more brutal than myself. But in this instance, it was with a boy almost as ineffectual with his fists as I was, and some bullying finally goaded me into losing my temper.

Carefully, the arrangements for the duel were made, not by ourselves, but between the leaders of the two gangs. It was to be at playtime in the afternoon. At the appointed time the playground fell silent, we carefully took off our coats, handing them ceremonially to our seconds, and then gingerly we both removed our spectacles: a de-vestiture that the rest of the boys witnessed with awe, for were we not now strangely handicapped for the business of battle? For each of us in our dazed state, there was small chance of vicious conflict, as we pawed the air to little effect. Finally, emboldened by what I found a surprisingly painless encounter, I jabbed at my opponent's face. More startled than hurt, tears came to his eyes. He tried to jab back, but I was quicker of foot, and with his first tears I was already the moral victor. The bell saved us both, but I found myself treated with a new respect.

It was my misfortune to be made to share my desk with a bossy, red-haired girl. These desks were designed to seat two, and it required mutual consent to raise the long desk lid. This consent was seldom forthcoming — from either of us. A daily battle ensued. My final resort was to pull her long red hair, a practice for which I was often caned. Nobody seemed to think of shifting me to another desk, although I wanted to sit by my friend Tommy Smith, a quiet boy but always smiling and as unaggressive as myself.

After initial difficulties, I had immensely enjoyed the Infants School, charmed by the colour, the delightful teaching, the toy town atmosphere of the classroom, with its plasticine, coloured blocks and counting beads, appropriate seasonal decorations, models of Father Christmas, Guy Fawkes, the gypsy caravan. Being already able to read and write I could give my time to the many delights, and all was sweetness and light. But alas! At the end of one summer holiday it was time for the Junior School. My difficulties of adjustment were aggravated by the fact that I arrived a week late, having been holidaying in London during a lull in the air raids, so everyone else had got over the strangeness and settled in. In addition, I had been placed in the second class, jumping standard I and the matronly care of Miss Hobbs, from which point of departure there were only men teachers, whom I did not like. My mother accompanied me on that first day, with excuses for my late arrival. I proudly wore over my shoulder my Mickey Mouse gas mask, so named because the gas mask was enclosed in a colourful tin depicting a Mickey Mouse saga in many colours. It had been purchased in Selfridges, and its vivid scenes impressed the class.

I cannot think we learned very much, but Mr Bevan's class proved exhilarating. It was generally agreed by us that he had been shell-shocked in the first world war, and this accounted for his entertaining and delightful ways as a teacher. Certainly he was much devoted to songs of the first world war, and we spent long, riotous and happy afternoons singing together — 'Sweet Rosy O'Grady', 'It's a Long Way to Tipperary', 'Goodbye Dolly, I Must Leave you' — these were his favourites and often, carried away by our joyous singing he would do a little dance himself in the front of the class. He told vivid stories of the war, enlivened by his gift of mimicry. I cannot remember that he was ever angry, or once told us to be quiet — except when he was marking the register, the one traditional school ritual he obeyed.

In Mr Bevan's care began my interest in reading and poetry. The latter began when he read us 'The Cow':

The friendly cow all red and white

I love with all my heart,
She gives me milk with all her might
To eat with apple tart.

They seemed to me the most marvellous words ever, and haunted my childhood. I was so impressed on that first hearing, in the drab, green-walled classroom, that I stuffed the poetry book up my jumper and nervously marched from the classroom at the end of afternoon school, clutching the magic volume. The theft was not discovered, and I ran home with mounting excitement.

Mr Bevan's favourite stories were of 'Just William', in which we too delighted, and with one of these we ended morning school. Eager for more I joined the library at the nearby Miners' Institute. The shelves, though dusty and in the limited care of a disabled miner, whose bronchial cough always warned of his approach, were rich in finds for any who would climb the rickety ladders to the lofty book cases. I was a constant visitor, and we became friends; for there were few regular readers now in the excitement of war, and the years of determined self-education and passionate religious and political debate were fading. Being left free of any homework at Junior School, I had hours available for reading. By the time of entry to the Grammar School, I was exploring the stories of Stevenson, Rider Haggard, Conan Doyle, as well as the 'Just William' series. Then, alas, the discipline of blinkered study began. I was on the academic tram-line. As well as this new lack of leisure time, the library at school also cut short my delight in reading fiction, for it offered only such writers as Jane Austen, George Eliot, the Brontes, Thackeray. At eleven years old they were offered and issued without introduction or thought about their suitability. They presented worlds remoter than the myths and tales of Greece and Rome and were certainly less exciting. I was soon bored, though I regularly took out a book monthly — we felt the English teacher would be appropriately impressed by such action — and by the second year at the Grammar School I had lost the habit of reading for pleasure, this being replaced by the more dubious blindfold passion for study.

But to return to the endlessly diverting Mr Bevan waltzing in front of the class while we sang 'Sweet Rosy O'Grady' and using his cane as partner. He taught all subjects except Welsh. For that most difficult of lessons we went one long afternoon a week to Mr George Smith a didactic unsmiling man who worked conscientiously through the Welsh Grammar book, while we sat, heads down, staring at the meaningless pages, nervous he might ask us to reply to one of the questions. Endless afternoons passed in parrot-like recitation:

'Ble mae'r pencil? Where is the pencil?'

'Dyma'r pencil. Here is the pencil.'

He held his pencil aloft. Tony London had a field-day at the back of the classroom with his alternative display. By the end of Mr George Smith's deadly pedagogic year we had progressed to:

'Ble mae'r ffenestr? Where is the window?'

'Dyma'r ffenestr. Here is the window.'

How we longed for Mr Bevan's dramatic telling, indeed performance, of the story of Gelert, that faithful hound stabbed unjustly by his impatient master, Llewelyn, a redoubtable Welsh Prince famous to us because of this tragic tale. We never tired of hearing it, the class always agog at the moment Llewelyn returned from hunting and killed the dog who'd safely guarded the baby from the predatory wolf, Gelert's victim, lying dead beside the safely cradled child. Beddgelert was the one place in Wales we longed to visit, leading Gyp reverently to Gelert's grave. Mr Bevan invited us to tell the story ourselves in our exercise books, and to supply a title. 'The Faithful Hound', 'An Heroic Dog', 'Brave Gelert' were favourite titles. Tony, the evacuee from London, in his 'ewn' fashion, a useful word that for us meant a rather pushy cheek and sauciness, not to say irreverence on this occasion, suggested 'A Typical Welsh Error' and 'It's a Dog's Life!' The story was usually followed by our singing Welsh folk songs together, both sad and rousing, as Mr Bevan delightedly conducted his joyous choir. Our favourite was 'Oes Gafr Eto' ('Here's another goat') which celebrated the counting of the goats, colour by fantastic colour, so that each chorus was introduced by a new hue — glas (green), coch (red) or whatever exotic shade caught Mr Bevan's fancy. Its bravura chorus we sang with total happiness. Equally rapt we sang the local folk song of the lowly thatcher in love with a young maid, daughter of a landowner and too far above his station for marriage: 'Bugeilio'r Gwenith Gwyn' ('Watching the white wheat'). The haunting and yearning melancholy of its notes filled those cheerful and bewitching afternoons, so different from language drills. The spell of Mr Bevan's magical classroom, and of the doomed romantic tryst we sang of, a bitter-sweet tristesse adolescence would later teach, was never to leave us.

Will Hopkyns' name was commemorated on the stone monument, surmounted with a Celtic cross, in the nearby hill-top village, facing on one side the pub, on the other the churchyard. Unlike Gelert's distant grave it was a memorial long familiar, but like the weed-grown and shiny graves beyond the church-wall kept for us truths other than those history or scholarship taught.

But alas, in George Smith's classroom the recitation of word-mutations and to us dull question-and-answer parroting seemed to go on for ever, no escape until the bell rang to end this monotony, and we could run back joyfully to the smiling presence of Mr Bevan, now no doubt sadly waltzing alone in the childless classroom.

The scholarship class was in the charge of Hopkin Bream, and 'Fish' brought an appropriate seriousness to the final year in the Junior School. His teaching consisted of ignoring most of the class, gathering round his desk the half dozen more-or-less dedicated souls whom he considered sufficiently industrious to attempt the scholarship examination. Nevertheless this did not entirely alter his morning routine. After solemnly marking the register, calling the names in dramatic voice and accent, Fish would instruct us to get on with our reading while he lovingly opened his morning newspaper. At the end of the first lesson Mr Smith would appear in the classroom, bringing his newspaper in exchange. Neither of them spoke while they exchanged papers. At the end of the second lesson it was playtime, and the moment for free milk distribution. Not until after morning break did Fish, both newspapers read, fully communicate with the class, silently reading or enthusiastically doing sums, heads down.

Due to the events of one momentous occasion, collection of the empty milk bottles was carefully supervised at the end of break by the class teacher. For the boys' organisation of 'operation piss-in-the-milk' was not to be soon forgotten by pedagogic authority. It happened while I was in Mr Bevan's class, and only just getting used to the tougher atmosphere of the Junior School. I had already been caned, once for talking twice in morning assembly, and on the other occasion by Mr Smith for hiding in the lavatory during his Welsh lesson. As a consequence of 'operation piss-in-the-milk' I was, for the first time, and together with every boy in the school, caned by the Headmaster.

The incident was provoked by Mr Harris-Hughes, who lived in a house facing the boys' entry to the school. It was his occupation to watch for any of us who might sneak out at playtime to buy sweets or hold a fight in the privacy of the street, and then report us, pointing us out to the master on yard duty. Feeling among the boys had been running high for some weeks, as Mr Harris-Hughes had been especially predatory, and a new teacher had been acting ruthlessly on these reports when on yard duty.

The plan was conceived in the communal boys' lavatory, the campaign centre of most of our plots since we were there free of prying masters and chattering girls. The place of origin also no doubt inspired the idea: each boy would, on the appointed day, quickly finish his milk at break time, secretly take the empty bottle to the lavatory, pee in it, then quietly place it on the window sill, door step, or pavement outside Mr Harris-Hughes' residence. We selected a Friday as on that morning he went up the town with his wife to shop. As a further precaution, all the boys agreed to drink lots of tea at breakfast; and some suggested, if possible, a bottle of pop each as that was much more effective.

'P. Day' arrived at last, the sun shone, and in the first two lessons there was a great restlessness throughout the school: some weaker bladders were constrained to ask permission to leave the classroom rather earlier; but fortunately we had hidden a few empty bottles behind the cistern the day before. At last the bell rang for break, and the operation was carried out with the precision and assured calm of a religious rite or military operation. No one spoke in the lavatory, each intent on his aim and his task. The excitement mounted as the hundred half pint milk bottles of pee stood sentinel on Mr Harris-Hughes' front door step, window sills, passageway, and also neatly lined the front wall of his house. The boys with greater capacity, and better aimers, contributed to the less full bottles.

As the sun shone down on the standing green and yellow-hued jars, we stared in fearful joy at the besieged, lonely house. Alas, the ringing of the school bell prevented our witnessing the arrival of Mr Harris-Hughes.

The milk monitors, the collection of milk bottles for the last time their responsibility, made the empty bottles from the girls, who sensed something untoward had happened but were banished at break time to their own walled yard at the opposite end of the playground, seem as numerous as possible.

Lessons began. Occasionally boys pleaded permission to leave, and returned with comforting reports of the scene at the front. It was during the fourth lesson, while Mr Bevan was leading us in rousing choruses of 'Ten Green Bottles Hanging on the Wall' at Tony's request, conducting with his stick, that the Headmaster burst into the room, his face the colour of the assembled bottles.

That afternoon, after a special assembly in the hall where we were harangued on our disgusting, just-like-animals behaviour, each boy received three strokes of the cane on his behind (I had never been caned there before), and the wretched milk monitors four, Fish and George Smith assisting in the onslaught while the girls gleamed with virtue and envy. Mr Harris-Hughes never reported anyone again.

Only once more did I enjoy the prestige of being caned by the Headmaster, and that was on the occasion of the 1945 General Election campaign, during my last weeks at the school. It was my first active involvement in politics.

Facing the school was an enormous wooden billboard, attached to the back wall of a house, and separated from the road by a garden and hedge. During the war it had proudly borne injunctions to salvage all waste, invest in war bonds, inquired 'Is your journey really necessary?', and carried heroic and vivid pictures of our soldiers in action against the enemy. With the coming of the election campaign, it bore an enormous picture of Winston Churchill, and the injunction 'Vote Conservative'. The war had become a civil one, the enemy our former but never in our world quite accepted battle leader. The readiness to reject was strangely easy, born also of home truths and bitterly remembered events.

To aim clodges of earth, which swooped over the protecting

hedge and bushes and sailed the whole length of the garden, preferably keeping up their line of flight until they hit the figure on the billboard, was no easy task for ten-year-olds. However, though the placard was regularly renewed, we managed to keep it permanently smudged, and on successful days of attack quite obliterated. Inevitably, the wall of the house also bore evidence of our mud-slinging, and the garden became a sea of clodges. Regular demands that this must stop were made by the Headmaster; there were daily canings for those caught. Soon we learned to operate only after school hours, and the final election result seemed the just reward for our efforts.

But already I was growing away from my friends of the street and the neighbourhood, a comradeship I was to lose entirely on my entry to the Grammar School in the 'posh' part of the town. In the two terms before the March Scholarship examination Fish was giving the few entrants his exclusive attention. I was happy to devote all my time to calculating the time it takes various drain pipes to empty baths, the cost per pound of bananas at £5 per hundred weight, to discovering the name given to a collection of witches or ducks or grasshoppers, divining the feminine form of fox or father, and writing innocent uncomprehending essays on 'When I Grow Up', 'Our Welsh Heritage', 'A Day in the Life of a Circus Lion'. I did not particularly miss the nightly company of the gang and their exploits — had I not always been a treacherous apostate, apt to break off relations and retreat to the pleasures of adult company at home? It was to become a total rupture, for my scholastic interests, already excited and satisfied by the dry material of examination cramming, became the sole occupation of my leisure time on discovery of the wider fields of History, Geography, Latin and French, Art and Science at the Grammar School. But these were gains at the expense of my awakening interest in literature, especially poetry, and my involvement with friends.

My grandmother was my assiduous tutor, as we joyfully worked through a series of Arithmetic books, 'First Aid in English' and the familiar, futile Grammar books. Suddenly my former play fellows seemed hostile, and I was subject to bullying, though as long as I didn't actually get physically hurt it troubled me little. There were the other joys of learning. But one boy, from another neighbourhood and whom I knew slightly, waited for me each day for two weeks as I left school, standing near the railings on the opposite side of the road, ready to inflict a quick stomach punch before he departed for home. Since I was a coward and not easily losing my temper, there was little to deter him, and he was sustained in this daily vigil, however long I lingered in the cloakroom or lavatory after school, by extreme patience and a deep ill-will. Then one day he wasn't there waiting, and afterwards while I remained at the Junior school he simply ignored me. An inexplicable and chance tormentor who, in later life, has appeared in different forms and in due course lost interest.

As we stood in our Socratic circle round Fish's desk one afternoon, answering Mental Arithmetic papers as he pointed to each of us in turn, he stopped, turned in my direction and said 'At this rate, you'll get all the answers right in the exam next week'. I was shocked with pleasure, having felt a poor runner beside the other candidates who boasted of their private coaching, at one shilling an hour, and were confident in its reflected security. But no doubt they lacked such a formidable pedagogic grandmother. Hearing my excited report of the tale she suggested that evening, after we had completed my Arithmetic answers and English essay, that I accompany her up 'The Lamb' in celebration of the compliment. Alas, how excellent the beer tasted and enjoyable the company of the gossiping women seemed in comparison to the rough, dangerous pursuits of the discarded boys of the street.

The day for announcement of the scholarship results at school arrived. Fish came proudly and open-mouthed, no doubt this time in genuine astonishment, into the classroom. Two of us had passed, and were instructed by him to go to the Headmaster's Room. I was fifty-fourth in the list of sixty-five who had passed. The other successful candidate was the one boy I had challenged to a fight. We walked, in new amity, to the Headmaster's Room.

The kindly Head instructed us, after congratulations, to go home and tell our parents immediately. I raced home, but it was still early morning, and my mother was up the market, and Granny still in bed. Never did I climb stairs more joyously, confident of the ecstasy on ascent. I burst into my grandmother's bedroom, where the brass knobs of the iron bedstead shone in the morning sun as never before, spluttering my breathless message. Granny, at that moment seated in her chair, her nightdress flowing about her, drew me to her and we kissed in a proud, clutching, fulfilled embrace. And in that sunny room began in earnest the quest where no grail awaits, that journey of discovery and alienation, the unquiet search for a spirit and a place where the burglars have not been.

Heydays and Holidays

Bank holidays meant the pit would be closed, and everyone took to drinking: it was a time of riotous parties, abundant food, and passionate quarrels. After closing hours some over-crowded boisterous households held their feuds in public in the street, while others watched from the doorstep, bedroom window, or standing near the scene of conflict. Language was violent, direct, and abusive, and the women, standing at their door, shouted their own case, and later, called their males to stop and come home to bed. The next day the feuding families, usually the same each holiday, were as amicable and devoted as ever. The air, and old grievances had been cleared, and they adjourned once more to the pub.

The first sign of the approaching bank holiday was the assembly on the kitchen table, together with a giant tin of Brasso, of the kitchen brass and copper ware: the six brass candlesticks that magisterially adorned the mantelpiece above the fire; the copper kettle; Gugga's silver cavalry stirrups that hung from the wall above; the triplex — now ornamental but from which the turkey had once hung and roasted before the fire at Christmas; the copper ash-stand beside the fireplace which was my special seat on long winter evenings when the coals grew red and the hazard-ous east wind belched back thick smoke into the kitchen. The elaborately wrought brass fender also received an extra special polish as did the oven and black-hob. Never early risers, our task wasn't started till the afternoon, so that meals were make-shift and abrupt on that day. But it didn't matter, it was part of the excitement, and I was usually allowed to assist with the shining of a candlestick until I spilt the Brasso tin. The cat, annoyed by this bewildering activity, miserably sought refuge under various chairs in the kitchen, only to be relentlessly disturbed as the cleaning caught up with him. Finally, surreptitiously, he would retreat to the parlour, and snuggle into my grandmother's fox fur which rested in solitary state on the plushest of the armchairs there. That retreat, too, would be eventually invaded as the cleaning progressed; but in the parlour this was a perfunctory dusting of the table, the Bible with a clasp in the centre, chairs, potted fern, and large, heavy-framed portraits of past family worthies in formidable Victorian dress, forbidding to behold. This room contained my grandmother's best furniture and was never used, except for terminal illness and funerals. Once you were sleeping in the parlour 'you were on the way out' as my impious father joked, and generally its atmosphere was that of an ante-room to death.

In later years it acquired a new role during the days before Christmas, when my father deposited there the poultry about to be sold, and I had to guard this sea of turkeys, chickens, ducks, legs of lamb and pork, and blood-stained furry rabbits, against the assiduous attempts at entry by the blood-scent intoxicated and wily cat. I sat there with a toy sword and in sailor's uniform, not liking the 'Little Boy's Soldier Outfit', monarch of all this edible and parsley-decorated flesh beneath the holly, paper decorations, and unnecessary mistletoe. On Christmas morning, the parlour now empty of meat, I would take my stocking of sweets, chocolates, and toys there, to play alone with these new riches, while the cat hovered distractedly between the smells of roast turkey in the kitchen and the stale odour of the now invisible carcasses in the parlour.

On his return from the market, my father often took the cat with him when he went 'out the back' to the lavatory at the end of the backyard. The cat enjoyed these outings, swathed in my father's recently bloodied meat-smelling butcher's apron. While my father read the paper there the cat snuggled in his blood-spattered nirvana. If afflicted with any every-day complaint my father would impatiently take the recommended medicament in one large dose. So he swigged the full bottle of syrup of figs one memorable Christmas Eve, having complained for some days of constipation. We saw little of him — or the cat — that festive time as they made their urgent pilgrimages 'out the back' in the seasonal falling snows.

With the approach of Christmas, when my endless scraps of paper scrawled with requests for toys were pushed up the sooty chimney, began the query from visiting aunts: 'What are you having for Christmas then?'

During the preceding weeks, Gugga had carefully and patiently schooled me to say 'Shit-house on wheels', and this I replied in totally serious and innocent voice and with all the child's solemnity and regard for the Christmastide. Though punished, bullied and warned by my mother not to give this reply, I protested that it was what Gugga had told me, and his word was truth. In any case he had trained me with Pavlovian thoroughness, and my retort was an automatic response. With visibly increasing nervousness my mother tried to cut short small-talk with such callers to the house as the rent man, who always left a shilling piece for me at this season, the insurance man, who was a chapel deacon, and in particular a prim young lady who collected weekly our subscriptions to the hospital fund: during these calls I was kept occupied in the kitchen. But it was during the visit of Aunty Caroline, who came from the socially ambitious, ostentatiously respectable side of the family that earned its living by the pen as insurance collectors and in minor clerical positions, and whose own husband had, in middle-age, received a call to train as an Anabaptist minister in West Wales, that all precautions broke down. It was a cold December day with a cutting east wind blowing and the night before the banshee had howled and whined around the backyard of the house.

I was sitting on the brass stand by the fire in the kitchen, secretly spitting on to the hot fender — for, unlike my grandmother, I could never reach the bars of the grate where the sizzling would be even more dramatic. My mother was mixing the Christmas pudding in the enormous china bowl from my grandmother's wash-stand upstairs, and Granny had gone up 'The Lamb' to fetch some beer for the mixture. We never much welcomed visitors from that side of the family, and Aunty Caroline could not have chosen a less convenient time. Perhaps my mother had forgotten my quietly spitting presence by the hearth, being engrossed in the accumulation of flour and peel and raisins and fat for the pudding. A few moments after Aunty Caroline had placed herself in the armchair — 'I never bother to make Christmas puddings now — I have them sent from Cardiff' — Granny arrived with a flagon of best Welsh bitter and several shiny sixpences for the mixture — the coins lucky finds in your Christmas pudding. 'I thought you'd be be too busy preparing for Christmas to call at a time like this,' Granny retorted, putting the flagon on the kitchen table, and Aunty Caroline visibly winced. She again explained, her accents even more rounded in the English way, that her Christmas puddings were coming from Cardiff. 'Dewi will be on carpet, soon, when he leaves Bible College!' said Aunty Caroline smiling, adding smugly 'He hopes to get a call to Barry. It will be nice there, by the sea, so much more relaxing and sophisticated than the valleys.'

'Dewi never had much stamina, did he?' grunted my grandmother dismissively, pouring some beer into the mixture. I had stopped my surreptitious spitting, enjoying the new scene. Aunty Caroline turned to me, and in her posh Sunday-school-superintendent-voice inquired, anxious to change the subject of conversation, 'And what is the dear little boy having for Christmas?'

'Shit-house-on-wheels,' I stolidly answered.

In the minute's shocked silence Granny winked at me and swigged the remainder of the flagon. White-faced, Aunty Caroline rose to go. 'I hope you all have a very happy Christmas. Give my good wishes to Uncle Jack. I must go — I promised to visit the children in hospital this afternoon. Such poor, dear little things.' She looked at me coldly.

After she went, I was allowed to put the new sixpences in the pudding mixture, and then Granny sent me up 'The Lamb' to fetch another flagon to celebrate, while my mother boiled the cloth-wrapped puddings in a boiler over the fire.

But the next Christmas, the family in London for the wedding of Aunty Delia, Gugga again delighted in subversive and festive comedy. He had briefed me that after I had recited the poem my grandmother had schooled me in for the evening wedding party, I must conclude: 'Now all you drunken buggers! Clear off back to Wales!' It was a five-year-old's party hit.

In later years, on entry to the local Grammar School, I nightly did my homework in the parlour, now transformed into a dusty firelit, lonely study. Unlike the front door, and the glass door that led from the tiled lobby to the passage, the parlour door was always kept firmly shut; so it was always something of a hermitage. When my concentration on Latin case endings flagged, I found it was wondrously restored by dressing in my grandmother's snug fox-fur, and enormous black straw, plumed hat.

Happily outré garbed I studied till the early hours oblivious of my bizarre appearance and passing time. Neighbours walking by who peered in must have wondered at the strange processes of education, but mine was not a reflective nature. In this past-haunted parlour, the shelves lined with my never-known aunt's untouched books, the hours of intellectual excitement quickly passed and the first burglars of loss entered. The leather-bound volumes and yellowing pages visit still.

Each bank holiday had its distinctive delights. Next to Christmas, Easter was my favourite. Each Good Friday morning, after the hot cross buns, came the familiar discussion.

'I wonder if they'll come from Ponty?' my grandmother would ask, though we all knew they would.

'Well I hope Aunty Dolly won't spend all the time quarrelling with Gilbert, like last year,' my mother replied. Dolly had done so last year, indeed every year that I could recall, and this quarrelsomeness with her son was a deep, articulate relationship.

'They'll visit the grave first, then call at 'The Old House', so they won't be here till stop-tap,' said my grandmother, putting on her coat and fox fur, pocketing her best silver snuff box. Good Friday was a market day locally, stalls and pubs busy, indeed the pubs uniquely open most of that holy day.

'Both will be drunk, and ready for a quarrel,' added my mother.

'Are you coming up "The Lamb"?' asked my grandmother. 'They'll probably call there first, after "The Old House".'

'No. I'd better be here when Tom comes from the market with the chops for his dinner. I hope he doesn't bring any of his cronies as well.'

'Can I come, Granny?'

'Well, you'll have to stay in the back kitchen. It'll be full up this afternoon.'

'And can I have some pop?' I knew I wouldn't in the end be

confined to the back kitchen, but secure in the beery holiday excitement of the middle room itself. And there was the arrival of Aunty Dolly to look forward to in the long afternoon of beer and gossip and singing, as the miners on this day drifted from the bar and joined their wives, festive and choral in the kitchen, as the middle room of the pub was called.

Aunty Dolly was an ancient, small, wizened woman, who wore steel-rimmed spectacles and always a black costume. I do not think I ever saw her sober, for she was always arriving at our house from the pub, carrying more drink, usually small bottles of whisky, in her handbag, while her son Gilbert clutched a frail of rattling flagons for later. She would return up 'The Lamb' the next morning immediately after a long, late breakfast of cups of tea, each with a drop of whisky in. Like my grandmother, she took snuff, but, as with beer, in more continuous and larger quantities. Her small silver snuff box she kept inside her heavy brown woollen stocking; and it was to my child's staring eyes fascinating to see her raise her skirt, peel aside her pink garter, lower her stocking, and release the snuff box, open it and, pressing her forefinger onto the soft, brown dust offer the box to my grandmother, saying 'Put your finger in, Florrie. It's the best quality. That old bugger Gilbert got it yesterday.' Then she would carefully return the box to its hiding place, only to begin the whole procedure again a few minutes later. My grandmother, less eccentric, kept her snuff box in her apron pocket. It was a sign that Dolly was very drunk when she fumbled and felt for her box in the wrong leg, cursing Gilbert violently and accusing him of having stolen it. Dolly had come from a well-to-do Cardiff family, who owned a large store there; 'They'd skin a flea for a ha'penny!' she'd declare. Her spick-and-span new valley house was much admired. Then, suddenly and Damascus-like, she took to drink, assisted by her grand inheritance. Cut off as the black-sheep of her family, she never looked back.

Her son Gilbert, named after her short-lived husband, was a tall, gaunt man in his fifties, with a high Roman forehead and bald head. He had served with gallantry in the first world war till taken prisoner, and would tell me how on returning home, and having his first bath for two years, his hair all fell out. I often tried to picture his entry into the bath-tub in the kitchen and the precise moment when his hair fell out, and scattered about him, but I never could quite focus the scene in my mind, and was never sure whether it was safer to bath very often or not at all. Gilbert, who had never married, was considered very intelligent, and in his youth, before taking to the bottle, had spent his leisure hours reading Marx, Engels and other political philosophers of the Communist Left. Following a visit there he was nicknamed Gilb Russia. He enjoyed discussion and debate at the Working Men's Institute, and was treated with grave suspicion by the Manager of the colliery where he worked, having had to move from our valley to Ponty because of victimisation. But his passion for intellectual study had now died, drowned by beer and political frustration, though when sober he would argue with my grandmother, for whom he was almost a match, and the air flamed with the clash between his Marxism and her Labour Radicalism, Robert Owen and Keir Hardie her particular heroes, while Dolly drank and fumbled for her snuff box. In the early hours of the morning, when they were all drunk and sentimental in the middle room, singing hymns and sad ballads Gilbert would sit beside the barrel installed in the cwtch, the dark, attic-like hideaway under the stairs that opened into the back-kitchen. Drunk but never festive, he would repeat prophet-like to himself, hour after hour and to whoever was there to listen, usually only me: 'Joe's the boy. Joe's the boy. The old world she'll split wide open.' I tried to understand the significance he obviously attached to Joseph Stalin, and knew only that he ruled Russia, a country most adults I knew spoke of with reverence and sympathy. More vividly I tried to visualise the world splitting open, while to Gilbert's oracular 'Joe's the boy. Joe's the boy. The old world she'll split wide open', I fell asleep beside the barrel, clutching the enormous jug from the wash-stand upstairs, which it was my duty to fill from the barrel and dispense to the ever-emptying glasses of the merrymakers.

Next morning, over her late whiskied-tea breakfast, Aunty Dolly would curse Gilbert, who seldom went to bed, falling asleep in his chair beside the empty barrel. But he had always left for the pub before she was up.

'The drunken bugger. He's gone again. Wait till he comes back, I'll kill the bugger.'

My grandmother tried to calm her.

'He's only gone with Jack up the Club. You know he likes to meet old friends.'

'The drunken bugger. Wait till I get him.' But by his return, she was sufficiently drunk to forget his morning treachery. Boozers together down the years, her constant fear and jealousy was that her son had, craftily, got in that extra drink more than she, and over their common pursuit they wrangled with the ferocity and devotion of lovers. But on Sundays in Ponty, pubs shut, they devotedly changed armchairs through the long afternoons and evenings, 'it makes a change' their mutual words of thanks as they moved either side of the fireplace, Dolly clutching her snuff-box and Gilbert his political tome.

I sat in the kitchen of 'The Lamb', between my grandmother and Aunty Martha, full of pop and crisps, as the hands of the clock inexorably reached four-thirty, half an hour after stop-tap. When I saw Titus and Gwen usher the drinkers from the bar, call time, and lock the pub, drawing the curtains so that the kitchen friends could continue drinking in comparative safety, I knew Aunty Dolly must again arrive soon as the other pubs would now be truly shut.

'I expect they went to see the grave first, and called at the pub up there,' said Aunty Martha, speaking of the hillside churchyard and the neighbouring pub.

'No doubt,' replied my grandmother.

'You know what Dolly's like,' added Titus, smiling down to his fat belly, 'she wouldn't pass "The Lamb", with Bill buried so near.'

'I remember it well,' reminisced Martha, 'he died seven days after Will. Dolly and me have been widows these thirty years.'

Suddenly, but without surprise, we heard a loud banging at the pantry window.

'You haven't shut the gate, have you, Titus,' asked Gwen, 'how can Dolly get in?' The large wooden, barred gates guarded the pub's yard and stable.

'Well, you've got to watch the law on holidays,' said Titus apologetically, rushing to open the back-yard gates.

'It's all right, I've got the tea-tray ready,' added Gwen, hopefully.

Dolly entered, her handbag heavy with bottles, dishevelled and rather drunk, Gilbert at her heels, solemn and holding his beer.

'We've only come to tidy the grave, Florrie. I'll be buried in Llan, if I have to walk there.'

It was the usual half-apologetic remark, the visit excused by the need to see her husband's grave, as though the thought that it provided also a change of scene for her drinking had never occurred. Dolly always added 'I'll be buried in Llan, if I have to walk there.' She turned to Gilbert, as if to emphasise her desire to be buried near her old home, 'and don't forget that, you drunken bugger — There'll be enough left for you all to have a drink up,' she added, waving her handbag to the assembled friends, 'but I'll be buried in Llan if I have to walk there.'

'Sit down, lovely girl,' said Aunty Martha fondly.

'Go on. Get us all drinks,' she ordered Gilbert, as though the pub had just opened. 'I'll be buried in Llan if I have to walk there,' she reiterated like a prayer or blessing, eyeing my grandmother uneasily.

'Put your finger in my hole. It's the best,' Dolly invited, bringing her snuff box to light.

'No, try mine,' said Martha, whose box was more quickly surfaced.

So the afternoon became evening drinking, and I sat quietly as possible, fascinated, hoping my grandmother would forget my bed-time, Aunty Dolly insisting on buying me a glass of shandy whenever her round came. Clearly I no longer needed the life-saving brandy!

The Golden Hatchets

Will-golden-hatchet and Dai-bit-of-cord lived in the house opposite us. They were miner brothers who had never married, for as Will-golden-hatchet would declare, he liked to 'put his feet under Mam's table', and indeed her roasts and fruit tarts would have kept many a man a hearty-eating bachelor, his flames of sexual ardour quenched by the sweet and savoury smells of cooking that permanently filled Mam's warm, womb-like but clean and spruce kitchen, the red coals of promise always bright in the grate. As she contentedly and lavishly cooked her only comment was 'I love to see a man eating!'

Mam's kitchen was the nearest thing we knew to a restaurant, and when she baked bread on Tuesdays we would play around the always open front door which led directly into the kitchen, savouring the smells of the baking bread and confident-in-hope of a crust, thick with salt farm butter and home-made goosegog, blackberry, or whinberry jam.

We told the days of the week by Mam's special dishes, for there was always, in addition to the usual meats and pies and fruit tarts, boiled ham on Wednesday, faggots and peas on Thursday, laverbread and cockles on Friday, Welsh cakes on Saturday, and broth on Monday. Only on Sundays did the other kitchens of the street smell inviting. Denied a hungry brood of grandchildren by the unflinching devotion of her two boys, irreversibly tied to the silk strings of her apron, Mam always enjoyed making a little extra of her special dishes for the favoured of her neighbours' youngsters.

Tales were told underground of the Trimalchian delights that Will-golden-hatchet and Dai-bit-of-cord drew from their capacious food tins at the shout of 'Grub up!' Famished young miners were always ready to help out Will and Dai if they were handling a tricky coal-seam in the first hours of the shift. 'Enough for a funeral!' was the familiar and awe-struck commendation of their

94

tightly packed food boxes. But while Will was always ready to share his food box with a hungry friend, never would he lend his meticulously cared for tools, especially his shining hatchet; and equally generous with Mam's sumptuous picnic — 'You can't see it, boys, but you can smell the bloody food as soon as the tin's opened' — Dai's parsimony led to frequent requests for 'a bit of cord'.

Their legs securely and fatteningly rooted under Mam's table, Will's and Dai's chief interests were divided between the chapel, their pigeons, and their allotment where their green fingers grew the vegetables Mam expertly cooked. In their back-garden, too, they cared for the chickens and the ducks who swam and quacked in the brook that ran at the far end of the garden. At the top end, nearer the house, stood the high pigeon shed, with its babbling and cooing on long summer days, as the brothers squatted and waited for return flights. On those warm days and evenings I listened and watched, too, in almost as fascinated and rapt attention as our patient, pondering, predatory old tabby Tiger. All the years of his life Tiger daily observed, padded over, brooded on that unenterable heaven, sometimes seemingly dozing but one green eye ever alertly open, and driven to such neurosis that some days he ignored all mice and men, even barking dogs, padding about the house a feline mystic, abstracted and vague, like the jealous God of legend and history knowing something we didn't.

Being chapel-goers and non-drinkers the Golden-hatchets were of course considered a very respectable family, and, it was rumoured, with 'a tidy bit of money'. Their only extravagance — and that in later years — was the installation of a telephone, an event which gave them exemplary standing in the street. The phone was kept on the small windowsill of the little-frequented front room, and seemed to be used by them only to trace and map the journeys and wanderings of their more pilgrim pigeons.

It took some time for them to adjust to the new machine, and in his excitement Dai was apt to pick up the receiver on hearing the phone ring, hold it as though it were likely to come alive in his hands, and then in his ever-mounting excitement on hearing the voice at the other end call to Mam in the kitchen, in confusion and elation replacing the receiver while she cried 'Don't dab it

down, Dai! Don't dab it down now!' hurrying from her steaming
kitchen and wiping her hands on her apron. Often 'Dammo!'
lamented Dai 'I've dabbed it down!' Sometimes 'I've beat him!'
he rejoiced, brandishing the receiver aloft. 'Don't dant Dai!'
encouraged the boys underground 'You'll beat the bugger before
long!' But 'I'm danted!' confided Dai, tearfully.

Nevertheless, the telephone gave a new dimension to their
public lives, for they were thrilled to receive messages for all
neighbours. Mam shouted to Dai not to dab it down while Will
raced to fetch the neighbour called for. It soon became a hot line
to the Doctor. At ten o'clock when they went to bed, a piece of
black velvet was ceremoniously and delicately placed over the
telephone, and it stood, a silent and draped sentinel in the dark
parlour window, even more wondrous to behold in this solemn
night attire as we stared through the undrawn curtains. And often
beside it a carefully written card 'Call in if you expected a call.
Dai dabbed it down.'

When we sang the popular Sankey hymns and choruses at
Florrie's parties, a barrel of beer in the cwtch to keep the bonho-
mie flowing, I especially loved the rousing verses of:

Telephone to glory, O joy divine.
I feel the current moving down my spine
O my God, the father, through the blood alone
A little talk with Jesus on the royal telephone.

And it was always Dai's telephone I pictured, assuming it was
directly linked with these hymned, celestial delights. But teetotal
and far too respectable, the Golden-hatchets didn't attend my
grandmother's convivial gatherings, to them saturnalia of the
golden calf. Leading members of the chapel choir, where Will's
counter-tenor was famed and treasured, the two brothers flour-
ished in the choral life of the valley, respected beyond thought or
breath of criticism. Though of course they were known under-
ground for a certain pennypinching and meanness — Will in his
absolute refusal to lend his hatchet, and Dai's constant cadging
of a bit of cord to tie the legs of his trousers. They were very private
individuals, and alone of the colliers refused to use the pithead
baths newly installed after nationalisation of the mines, building

a rough bathroom of their own in a lean-to that adjoined Mam's busy back kitchen.

But alas, the harmony of their little house, the calm of their Oedipal Eden was marred by their next-door neighbours, the noisiest and most shiftless family in the street. Adept at cadging 'a bit of tea in paper' or 'a drop of milk in this cup' and always 'on the minge', the Smiths were more familiarly known as 'the black arses' from Mrs Smith's habit of turning her backside to a neighbour after a quarrel, then abruptly raising her dress and sticking out her uncovered behind in insult before entering her front door. Against the Golden-hatchets they waged perpetual warfare, with breaks only for cadging, unforgivingly roused by their respectability and supposed wealth. On a day of high passions, Ruby Smith's tongue lashed them the whole length of the street, Mam Williams retreating to her kitchen, all doors firmly shut. But Ruby's battles with the packmen were the fiercest.

The packmen, who sold clothes and household goods at exorbitant and extortionate prices but who accepted payment at one-and-sixpence a week and would give a pound's worth of credit, came round late on Friday and Saturday afternoons when pay packets were full. It was a warm Saturday in July, and I was sitting on the edge of a chattering basket of pigeons, ready on the pavement for dispatch, Tiger Trojan-like in his attentiveness, but neurotically divided between the pigeon cot and the guarded basket. Will and Dai were busily and excitedly getting ready the second basket and awaiting the carrier. Ruby, in her apron, was leaning against the front door, declaring from time to time 'Thank God those bloody pigeons are going to shit somewhere else for a bit! Burn the cot down I will if they keep me awake any more.' Will and Dai pretended not to hear, and Ruby was so engrossed in her commentary of abuse and threat that the packman was at her door before she could run inside and bolt it against his voracious intrusion.

'Good afternoon, Mrs Smith,' grinned the packman, resting his bundle of wares on the pavement, 'a lovely day isn't it!' 'Fourteen-and-six behind you are with the payments', he added ingratiatingly but with threat. I looked up. Tiger still stared at the pigeon-box, and Will and Dai pretended not to listen.

Ruby stiffened glumly, and pulled straight her dress.

'I'd better have a bit off this week,' said the packman, still smiling. 'If you can manage it.'

'You'd better come in!' said Ruby. 'That drunken bugger isn't home yet.'

The door shut.

I ran my hands along the wickerwork crate. The pigeons fluttered. Tiger shivered with excitement.

'She's drawn the bedroom curtains,' whispered Dai, excited too, and ran in to tell Mam.

Unable to contain himself any longer, Tiger leapt on top of the pigeon shed. I poked my finger through the wicker bars of the crate.

Half-an-hour later I looked up from the babbling box to see the packman scurrying up the road, a breathless Autolycus. A moment later Ruby rushed out onto the pavement.

'Come back, you flamer! Come back, you old bugger!' She turned to Will and Dai, unaccustomed allies, and only just emerged from the safety of Mam's kitchen. 'Wait till I see him next week!' Then to the street she shouted — 'And he's only taken a shilling off', waving her payment book at the fleeing packman, while the love-pigeons cooed.

'Well, you don't miss a slice off a cut loaf' declared my grandmother, hearing of the episode in the pub that night, while I drank my uncomprehending glass of shandy beside her.

Days For The Queen

Our own life style was generally less crowded with incident than many in the street, and certainly more private, apart from the occasional day trips to the seaside in summer and of course the daily strolls up 'The Lamb'. For my Aunts the annual chapel excursion to Aberavon by pony trap was the highlight of the year. Then the first rail excursion occurred, and that on a Sunday; nor was it a chapel outing.

The Old Testament-like black-coated figure on the crowded and excited platform added a special drama to the happy occasion. It was Jenkins Bethania. His rather grand Victorian villa, Bethania House, with its french doors opening on to the front lawn and its glass-roofed covered way that led down steep steps to the garden gate — like many houses in the town it was built on a slope — we could see across the river from our back-bedroom window. We often watched Jenkins Bethania practising his Sunday sermon marching up and down the lawn, sometimes disappearing under the covered way as though into a special holy place, his locks of flowing grey hair askew. That we could not hear his actual words added to the spell he cast, his arms in dramatic and melodramatic gesture, no doubt castigating our sins and casting out devils. But his historic railway platform performance could be both seen and heard by the multitude, green hillsides along the track bright in the hot sun of August, though there was no burning bush. Catching sight of one of his own flock, in a voice of summer thunder before the storm, he spoke: 'If you go on this outing to Porthcawl on Sunday you are going to Hell, Bryn Bevan! To everlasting Hell fire!' 'It's all right, Reverend Jenkins, don't you worry, I've got a return ticket,' Bryn confidently replied, as the packed and joyous train departed. Unabashed, Jenkins Bethania held a small prayer-meeting for the souls of those driven by the whips of pleasure that August Sunday to sunny Porthcawl, joined by those who'd come to wave goodbye. Later in the war years when faced by an irate customer in the market stall who'd spied a leg of Welsh lamb under the counter, Morgan would quell immediately all appeals from the waiting women in the angry queue with his punch line: 'Sorry, love, can't sell that, it's for Jenkins Bethania', though the Inspector of Police was the likelier lucky recipient. More maritime, our Minister had baptised his flock in the river, which he called Jordan tides, dipping white-clad maidens in the holy streams, in Arcadian, sylvan rites.

Today was a warm August one too, though a modest coal-fire burned in the grate, for such domestic uses as cooking, warming my grandfather's bath water, and heating my grandmother's curling tongs. It was my job to see there was always a full bucket of lump and one of small coal, fetched from the coal-house at the bottom of the garden, and kept under the old wooden table in the yard, sheltered from the worst of the rain. 'Mind the house' was my grandmother's stern command as they all went up 'The Lamb'. 'And if the insurance man calls say "Come next week. The money's in the jug upstairs! They're up 'The Lamb'".' I enjoyed minding the house, as I could sit on the brass-stand by the fender and spit into the red coals. It was exciting to miss, for then the spit sizzled as it hung from the bars of the grate. I early learned to keep the fire going, first with lumps then banked with as much small coal as possible without actually douting the fire, so that wisps of thin blue smoke usually drifted up the chimney, often violently blowing back when there was an east wind and filling the kitchen with acrid blue smoke. One August bank holiday, alas, when my mother was up the market and Granny up 'The Lamb', I neglected my task. Unnoticed the fire went out. It was a hot afternoon, the sun streaming through the kitchen window, when Dolly and her son Gilbert arrived from Ponty, taking advantage of the weather to inspect the grave. Dolly burst in, her handbag rattling with small whisky bottles, and noticing the dead coals in the grate said: 'Let's go, Gilbert! Back to Ponty! No fire, no welcome! There's not a flame in the grate! No fire, no welcome!'

'Gran's up "The Lamb",' I said, trying to divert the attack. Aunty Dolly rose to go, sweating profusely in the sun-filled back kitchen. '*You'd* better come up "The Lamb",' she said, glaring at the grate of ashes.

As we left, Sophia, sitting on her front doorstep in the unaccustomed warmth, asked if she could borrow my grandmother's catalogue, to leaf through its pages of cheap coats and dresses, skirts and blouses, on this afternoon of dreamy summer sunshine, street-neighbours sitting outside in relaxed, balmy, gossiping amity. I ran back to get the catalogue from its special place in the middle dresser drawer, amid Granny's account books, invoices, and scribbled order notes. She usually devoted an hour to it each afternoon, my special task to take the large brown order and payment envelope to the post office, 'I'll count how long you'll take' her signal for me to set off. I returned breathless to the count of 'three hundred and ninety two' or a similar striking figure, never doubting its accuracy or the faithfulness of her count as I ran the streets with a boy's total conviction and purpose.

The back-kitchen was in full session, the window into the street a little open for the sun, Aunty Martha tiptoeing a little dance in the narrow passageway to the bar, cradling an empty Guinness bottle in her arms, far gone. Returning to her armchair by the fireplace she announced:

'I'd like a stauncher! I'd like a stauncher!' bending her elbow and jabbing forward her forearm. 'No taste of copper, ladies!' beamed Titus, bringing a free round.

'I've been suffering from the pethic, all day,' lamented Evan the Milk.

'What's the matter?' muttered Jinny, sipping her Guinness.

'It's all right, love, I'm only a bit pethic, only a bit pethic,' babbled Evan, a tear running down his plump, red face, and settling on the rose in his buttonhole. 'Everybody isn't painted with the same brush,' condoled Jinny. They made way for Aunty Dolly. Gilbert had gone into the bar.

'Can we stay tonight, Florrie?' asked Dolly, forgetting the empty grate.

'It'll be a good night,' replied Florrie in assent. 'We're playing a team from the Cape. Show Aunty Dolly your poster,' she said to me. 'You can ask Titus for it — it's in the bar.'

The ladies' darts team had been going for a year now, and it was my happy task to make the poster that announced forthcoming matches, and to keep the scorebook. The team from the Cape was a festive one, and the younger men supporters called me 'wus', joking with me 'Keep off the beer, wus, if you're scoring!' It would be a good night, and this was only the afternoon session. 'Let's have "Freddie Welsh",' said Jinny to Bob Ponty, a gentle, humorous man who'd lodged with his wife Bet in Jinny's front room since their midnight flit some years ago from Pontypridd. Occasionally Jinny would grumble about the noise of their wireless, and Bet would angrily declare to the kitchen friends 'If Jinny complains again I'll set it free! I'll set it free!' But the plug in the wall remained, rented from the local wireless shop, Dai Plug's. Now Bob Ponty was to be the first performer. He was already on his feet, introducing with comic dancing movements and mock pugnacious fists his own special song:

> To beat Freddie Welsh, the boy,
> Wales' pride and joy,
> You've got to be very clever to beat that Ponty boy.

'Now Delia, let's have *your* Ponty song,' requested Jinny after Bob's acclaimed turn. My Aunty Delia had spent several miserable years in service in London, homesick most of the time and though valued because she was a tireless worker, had been uncomfortable in the snobbish, pretentious house where she served. Happily home on holiday, her song too was presented in comic spirit.

> Oh Mam, can I come home!
> Oh Mam, can I come home!
> Send me one-and-ninepence,
> My fare to Pontypridd
> And I'll walk the rest back home!

At the end of the afternoon session it was only the kitchen friends who could remain to enjoy Gwen's ham and cheese sandwiches, stayed now with cups of strong tea, surreptitiously laced from Dolly's handbag bottles.

'Cut your coat according to your cloth,' declared my grandmother after a tale of extravagance by a neighbour. 'Pisin berwi

— mutton dressed up as lamb!' was Jinny's caustic aside. 'Her mother would turn in her grave,' said Martha, a proposition so often made at some folly or fecklessness, whether financial, moral or sexual, that I sometimes had a surreal vision of a cemetery of mothers spinning in their pious graves.

'Look at Ben!' said Jinny. Ben had been a sailor and after a few drinks simply exclaimed 'Banbury Fair! Banbury Fair!' his eyes bright with remembrance of youthful adventures, but he never yielded more precise detail despite the women's teasing inquiries.

'He always was a hobbledehoy,' added Martha, warming up to the attack on her fey neighbour, 'and he's been on the randy all the week!'

'An old one closing is as good as a young one opening,' said Dolly drily.

'Not like Gander,' added Jinny wistfully, for Gander used the next-door front room as the local barber shop. He was a tall handsome Italian who mostly cut hair on tiptoe, for he was always trying to watch the street's comings and goings, peeping above the net curtains that guarded the privacy of his barber's shop from curious passers-by. Gander's craning neck was itself a street spectacle.

'We'll all be pushing up the daisies before long!' was my grandmother's dismissal of the topic. And pushing up the daisies was the phrase that held our notions of an after-life, its pastoral energy half humorously affirming common thoughts on mutability.

'Go and tell your mother the dart match is starting on the dot of seven,' instructed my grandmother, and on my slight hesitation, for I was happily lapped in the women's love and gossip, added 'it's only a heck and a calm to the bottom of the street.'

'He's an old soldier,' said Martha fondly as I left, and I heard the rattle of teacups and plates being collected up by Gwen. My grandmother adjusted her fox fur and took out her silver snuff box, at her post for the evening's activities.

'Five-to-six, Titus! It's time for the first round!' Opening her purse, 'It's a day for the Queen!' she declared with republican fervour and contentment.

'The apple doesn't fall far from the tree,' muttered Dolly, finishing off her whisky tea.

Already far gone and draining her whisky, 'Fuck your friend,' confided Jinny to her freshly frothing half of bitter.

'Love goes like the rainbow,' said my grandmother, raising her first glass of the evening. And war took love and rainbows, however fast we held.

Yearly Dolly had inspected the grave where in time she was laid, though she survived Gilbert by a year. He died of cancer, and as he lay wasting away refused all food with the proud declaration 'I'll starve the bugger. That'll kill him.' His will left express instructions, and £30 for all his friends, to drink up up 'The Lamb' after the burial. It was clear Aunty Dolly would not last long, there was no-one now to drink with, nor to engage in fierce, loving filial squabbles. Her vitality and will to live poured with the rain into her son's thirsty grave. 'Gilbert is calling me,' she declared for eleven lonely, uncomprehending months, visiting us still on each bank holiday, and on the twelfth joined him.

For the first time I saw my grandmother weep, and the days grew darker as winter and war approached.

The War

The coming of the war brought many new excitements, and only a vague, distant, ever present but remote danger. The killing, the blitz, the separations, the wounding and dying was happening somewhere else. We heard of it on the news, and there were accounts and pictures in the papers. No close relations were in the forces; so the worst of war really belonged to other people.

Rationing, to our family, brought its discomforts rather than distresses, and even those were the shortage of such luxuries as bananas, chocolate, biscuits, grapes. During the war I was haunted by the absence of bananas. I always seemed to be seeing pictures of them in books, and the episode of Ben Williams and the bananas highlighted my wartime years.

Somebody's relation had returned from, it seemed to me, at least the South Seas, and brought a bunch of six bananas. These were presented to the Headmaster of the Primary School I attended. At morning assembly they were held aloft by the Headmaster, to our admiration and awe. By this time, we had forgotten the physical touch and taste of bananas. They belonged to the world of fantasy and magic. These were to be raffled, for the war effort. And each day, at assembly, after the prayer, the Head would hold them aloft as we fingered in our pockets the pennies that would enable us to buy further raffle tickets that day. This bunch of bananas had assumed enormous proportions in our minds and imagination: nothing seemed so marvellous to behold, possession of them intimated joys beyond the imagination. No one really believed they could possess them: purchasing the ticket was an experience that excited possibilities of divinity. The requests sent up by each child during morning assembly's silent prayer were one great hope.

At last the Friday afternoon of the draw arrived, and the whole school was assembled. I nervously fingered the twenty-seven tickets in my pocket as the Headmaster spoke at great length of the war effort to which our pennies would flow. Finally, in a total quiet unique in the history of the school, the draw was made by the Deputy Headmistress with a delicacy that would have pleased Damocles. The name of Ben Williams was called. And Ben, a quiet and a solitary dark-eyed boy from the very next street, was called to receive the golden bananas from the Headmaster. And until we left the Primary School Ben was treated with awe and respect, the one who had won the bananas, though in moments of hostility between gangs the name sometimes shouted was 'Ben Bananas' but this seemed only to add to his stature as the shouter of the taunt remembered that heroic day.

It was the building, or rather the long non-building of the air-raid shelters, that really brought the war home to us. One day lorries arrived and deposited hundreds of bricks at the bottom of the road, near the brook, and on a neighbouring patch of waste ground. It was conveniently at the beginning of the summer holidays, and officially nothing further happened to the bricks for months. They soon became an inexhaustible source of amusement and play.

The great game was the building of what we called fairs, and though quite unlike the usual merry-go-rounds, they gave us weeks of excitement and diversion. This pastime consisted in arranging a continuous line of bricks in devious and winding patterns about the road, over the hedge, and into the waste plot. Each of us built our maze of bricks, devising ever more imaginative patterns. For the price of a few chinas — those bits of broken china we collected and hoarded as money, for they were the accepted means of exchange — you would permit friends to walk on the low wall of bricks you had devised, with its picturesque twists and turns, bridges and sudden elevations. With a new gimmick, like Freddie's building a bridge of bricks across the shallow but ever-flowing brook, you could, in one day, make a whole box of chinas. In war-time of course even broken china was sometimes scarce, and on a poor day, if I'd lost my previous pile of 'chinas', it was helpful to steal the odd cup and break it. Clean broken china, especially if it were coloured and illustrated, was especially valuable and worth two, sometimes three, pieces of plain white china.

After a few weeks the plotted walks we built with the bricks became even more involved and complex, often including a challenging water-jump, and a really high series of steps that gave that added delight of requiring a sense of balance in successfully walking along the barricade. Then, one day, we found some rusty zinc sheets left on the river bank, and built a den high enough for us to sit in. It became the meeting place of the gang until the men finally came to build the shelters. So then I buried my store of chinas in the garden, where they would be safe as a dog's bone till some future date when I needed them. But it never came.

It was when the shelters were built that Freddie, the leader of the gang because he was the biggest, the toughest and the most daring, came into his own. There were two brick shelters, each with a large, flat concrete roof, excellent for playing on. Between the two shelters ran a brick wall, about five feet high and easily scaleable. From the wall one could, with a little nerve and the right use of hands and feet in climbing, get on to the roof of either shelter. The builders, as though sensitive to the daring and dangerous delights of boys, had built one shelter three feet lower than the other. Quite soon Freddie demonstrated it was possible, with further nerve, to jump across from the roof of the higher shelter onto the lower one. As the intervening wall was lower than both shelters it was more a threat than an obstacle. At the end of the first week it was necessary to jump from one roof to the other even to be a member of the gang. In due course we all qualified. It was when trying to jump, practising alone one night in the half dark, from the roof of the lower up to the roof of the higher shelter that Freddie broke his neck, and his daring became blood and dust.

So we found other pursuits then, and had a new leader. Tommy Thomas was our new leader. He was almost as tough as Freddie, but less foolhardy and more cunning. As he lived very near me, I soon became second-in-command, also because, though Ken Griffiths was a better fighter, he wore even thicker glasses. If Ken misbehaved at home his mother wouldn't let him wear his glasses, so some days he walked short-sightedly about, blind as a bat, a total hindrance on the gang's escapades. After a while, however, when wearing glasses lost its novelty and distinction, he was always breaking them in fights and on our perilous adventures. So his mother decided he should wear them only to school and on Sundays. And it seemed, to Ken and ourselves, a reasonable arrangement. Though later he had special permission to wear them to the Saturday children's matinees, when 'Going to show?' the boys would cry on rounding up each of the gang. We saved sweet coupons all the week for our supply of pear-drops, bubble gum, liquorice allsorts. There was also a bottle of pop, either lemonade or dandelion and burdock. We picked the 'Ritz' because we could sit upstairs, in the front row if first in the queue. There we could lean over the balcony and gob on those sitting below, aiming a long, slow spit on the head far beneath. Sometimes we missed. Though once we were caught and chucked out. As it was a long way from the lavatory we could also pee on the floor if we did it quietly.

With the imposition of the blackout, the lamp-posts, now gaunt unlit pillars, lost their importance as the meeting places of the gang at night. We took over the new brick shelter, soon unhinging the door, and it seemed a most conveniently bestowed meeting-hall of our own. We armed ourselves with lanterns, made from joining together two tin cans with a jam pot for the centre part; and in this centre part we placed our stumps of candle. Carrying our 'Dici-show-light', as these homemade lanterns were called, we moved about the neighbourhood at night like shadowy, noisy glow-worms. And these errant 'Dici-show-lights', flickering candles against the night, gave a new depth and meaning to the dark. On evenings when we dressed up and played in strange, discarded and borrowed clothes, sang and shouted, pantomimed and quarrelled, moving in disordered procession about the street, it was a tattered world of carnival as our dici-show-lights briefly lit the wartime gloom.

My grandmother took pride in the possession of a rather fine, adult-made 'Dici-show-light'. Each evening, as she prepared for departure to the local, she carefully trimmed and lit the candle wick. Half way up the road she called in as usual for Aunty Martha, and together, guided by the candlelight, they slowly made their way to 'The Lamb'. They usually left about eleven, or after midnight if my grandfather was working overtime and not expected back; by which time the street was deserted and pitch black. Often I made pilgrimages from the fire-lit kitchen to the front door, spying for any sign from the wandering lantern at the top of the street. At last it would glimmer, moving in slow zigzag lines across the street, but inevitably nearing as with meandering, drink-giddy steps Granny and Aunty Martha journeyed in procession down the street, cursing the Germans and the dark, and sharing their brave candle in a naughty world.

Sometimes they were accompanied by Maggie, whose joy in life, at seventy, had been revived by the new spirit of defiance of the enemy that was abroad. It was during a heavy raid on Swansea that Maggie, given to acrobatics and dancing when adequately drunk, made her first gesture of defiance. It was one of the few nights when we actually heard, and some claimed they saw, the German bombers fly overhead. So we all retreated into the cwtch, the sloping cupboard under the stairs, sitting uncomfortably amongst the discarded bric-a-brac and clothes that awaited collection for salvage. In a sudden and unusual burst of comradeship we were joined by the cat, who purred with pleasure at this new communal home, his ultimate lair suddenly so popular.

But a few doors away, Maggie, whose husband worked nightshift in the nearby munitions factory, reacted otherwise. Dressed in one of her long, gypsy-like garments, complete with a bright beaded necklace and castanets, she had climbed onto the wooden kitchen table, and was spiritedly dancing there and singing 'Do you see me dance the polka?' while the green eyes of her four cats shone in the firelight. Peering through the undrawn curtains of the kitchen window, terrified by this strange vision illumined by the flickering light and shadows from the blazing coal fire, a lone air raid warden fled to the local and drank consecutive pints till the all clear sounded and his vision faded.

Unfortunately Maggie's husband was against 'the drink', and if her drinking sessions up 'The Lamb' went on till the early morning hours and he got home before her, it was his custom to bolt the back gate, though not the kitchen door, a curious gesture of half-protest. On such occasions, leaving the drinking party near dawn, Maggie took pleasure in the thought of jumping over the three-foot-high stone wall that surrounded their garden, a gymnastic feat at which she had grown adept, while her husband stubbornly snored in his single bedroom. Alas, one frosty dawn, she caught her foot while jumping, and fell into the yard, breaking her back. In a blaze of pain and defiance she died, surrounded by her dumb green-eyed lovers and the winter cold.

Like most commodities during the war, beer was in short supply and subject to a rough and ready system of rationing. The lorry carrying the large, breast-like barrels came to our local each Thursday. As the week's supply was usually exhausted by Monday, it was a day of anticipation and excitement, my grandmother ready for departure from mid-day.

It was my task to act as look out, taking up my position on our doorstep at eleven o'clock in the morning, usually the earliest time the lorry was expected. So I kept a careful eye on the top of the street, ready to rush in with the news the moment the lorry turned the corner and the draymen began levering the barrels from the lorry and down into the cellar of the pub. Within minutes my grandmother and I would be on our way up the street, indifferent to the silent and hostile stare of the respectable and morning gossips, standing on the pavement in clucking cliques.

As the landlord did not open the pub in the public absence of beer, the main doors were usually locked until the evening hours of opening, when the arrival of the beer was revealed to all. In the late morning on Thursdays my grandmother gave her usual secret code, three knocks on the pantry window, and Gwen hastened to let her in through the back gate, carefully locking it afterward. We were always comfortably seated in the back kitchen, which was the living room, where Gwen was preparing the dinner, by the time the draymen came in for the first draw from the barrel, which Titus was getting ready in the cellars. Titus, an enormously fat man with a bald head and three fingers missing since the battle of Vimy Ridge, was afraid of his shadow and especially of my grandmother and Aunty Martha. He would come up proudly from the cellar, sweating with effort and excitement to announce joyfully — by this time Aunty Martha with four taps on the pantry window had also arrived — 'two glasses, ladies?' It was the best half-pint of the week, and the draymen were tucking into ham and eggs.

On Thursdays nobody bothered to go home for meals, it was a waste of time, and once the pub was generally open to the public in the evening there would be savage inroads into the supply of beer. Soon several of the 'kitchen friends' were convivial over their glasses of bitter and the war seemed, indeed was at that moment, far away. And each week there was usually someone home on leave, a husband, nephew or son who joined the matriarchy, all by the evening sentimental with beer and choral with emotion. Often it was a service man stationed nearby, passing that way and glad for the warmth and welcome of the fabled kitchen friends, for war had already eased and diminished social and sexual boundaries. Near the time of preparation for the Normandy landings it was sometimes a lonely American who happened by, generous to me with chocolates and gum, and who was more interested in sentiment than sex, lulled by the brief security and company of this beery haven. In convivial song and anecdote — reminiscent or suggestive — around the warming flames of the fireside and mothering friends was revived a womb-like safe place. Titus served from his diminishing supplies with beaming pleasure, and Gwen cut sandwiches as the women proffered a few lumps of cheese, some slices of cold meat, the rare tin of spam, from the pockets of their flowered pinafores. They were happy and happy-go-lucky feasts. On Thursdays, too, we were joined by Evan the Milk, who finished his now-rationed round much earlier and brought his amiable old horse Dando into the pub yard to rest for the day. I liked the gentle, amusing Evan the Milk, who always had sweets, and wore a red carnation if we had won a battle, a white one in defeat. After three or four pints, he would proclaim 'I'm depressed, Mama' to my grandmother, and by his sixth was in continual tears, weeping into his handkerchief over specific but unnamed griefs and sorrows half enjoyed. 'I cried a bellyful, Mama, I cried a bellyful!' his favoured lamentation.

But there was one week, just one, when Titus rebelled. His son Glyn had trained as a teacher and went to live in England with his wife, never returning to the home he now looked down on — though Gwen treasured and would read aloud to us his infrequent letters. Glyn, a recently conscripted airman, was reported missing that week on a bombing raid. On Thursday Titus locked himself in the cellar with an old first-world-war crony, and for three days they refused to budge, till they had drunk all the beer, while Gwen wept in the back kitchen, lapped in the dry comfort of the sober women.

Soon afterward they decided to retire, broken in hope and spirit, to the remote village in the West of Wales whence they had come to the tumultuous upheavals of the mining valleys at the turn of the century, Titus in energetic pursuit of a miner's wage and work.

They left at the turn of the year, and the day before departure my grandmother declared a farewell party, the kitchen friends determined to snatch a last joyous comradeship against the parting of the ways and war-torn, bereft worlds. The next day Titus and Gwen departed, returning to womb or tomb, tenants of indifferent lives.

The Lights Go On Again

My grandmother and I were keen followers of the progress of the war, especially in Europe. Pinned on one of the kitchen walls was a large and detailed map of Europe, whose centre Germany filled like a spider — but it was an ever-decreasing web whose diminution we daily followed and plotted on the map. Over the war years we had modelled a collection of British, Russian and American flags, carefully fixed on to pins. With them, we marked the latest positions of the Allies on their advance through Italy, into France and across Belgium and Holland into Germany; and the march of the Russian armies from Stalingrad and into eastern Europe had equal pride of place. Though I was often up in time for the early morning news bulletins because of school, no flags were moved until my grandmother had herself listened to the afternoon dispatches and I had returned home. And then only after we had consulted the accounts and maps and diagrams in the daily newspapers — we took *The News Chronicle* and *The Daily Worker* — as an overall check. The adjustment of the flags, especially if an important new objective had been gained such as a town clearly marked and obviously significant on our wall-map of Europe, was the high point of the day's events. As the war in Europe moved inexorably towards victory, the map took pride of place in our kitchen and was much admired by visiting relations.

My favourite of these was my grandmother's sister-in-law, Aunty Bessie, a big, formidable, fearless woman who when a young girl had been briefly imprisoned for hurling a lump of coal at one of the mine managers during a tempestuous demonstration against a forced cut in wages. Those were times of industrial riot and unrecognised civil war. As Home Secretary, Churchill had ordered the use of troops against the striking miners, a poor, defenceless and hungry company — and it was a daily catechism, not forgotten in war. He was never for us a war hero. In the early forties, before the tide of war had turned in our favour, my Uncle Harry won fame for breaking the record in cutting and loading the most coal in a day's work. As coal was essential in our perilous stand against the Nazis, miners were heroes again, not the enemy within, and Harry's feat was a matter for national recognition and rejoicing. London journalists called at the house. There they were given short shrift. 'Changed your tune, haven't you, since the strike? You'll be back to your old ways no doubt, after the war,' declared Mary, shutting the door in their faces.

In old age Bessie's voice of protest had not diminished, but now she was more preoccupied with the approaching problem of death, sensing mortality with as keen a smell as she had nosed out bullying and victimisation by the predatory mine owners. Her first husband had been killed, buried alive during a pit explosion just after the First World War, and she still recalled, music to my eager ears, how the banshee had howled beneath the kitchen window for two nights before, its dreadful whine still as haunting to her as the white-shrouded remains. I hoped, though realising I was tempting the most terrible fates, I would hear the banshee, the particularly whining sound the wind sometimes made as it whipped down the mountains and about the house, but fortunately I never did hear it in its full fury. When a strike ended Aunty Bessie would announce 'They've gone back to work. I'll have an egg for my tea', scuttling out to the backyard chicken shed. But poverty ended with the war and consequent full employment.

Aunty Bessie had later married a small, lean-faced man called Will, who resembled a kindly fox, and her one plea, during her conversations with my grandmother, was that she might be spared 'till I put Will Williams away tidy, first. Then I'll go.' It had been a matter of great concern for her when the practice of women joining the column of male mourners walking behind the hearse to the cemetery for the burial was discontinued, especially as it was soon after that her own Aunt Phoebe, who lived to the age of ninety-four, died. Determined to ignore the custom of excluding women mourners from the graveside, Aunty Bessie had walked resolutely at the back of the procession of solemn, chapel-suited men, announcing every few yards as though to a roadside audience requiring explanation 'I'll see the last of my Aunt Phoebe ...

I'll see the last of my Aunt Phoebe.' And so she did. She was also spared, despite grievous surgery, 'to put Will Williams away tidy, first', and then contentedly died within the month.

A very different visitor was Aunty Sarah Bowen, much more preoccupied with the welfare of the living than the dead. Her husband too had been killed in a colliery accident, but she had not wanted a second marriage, turning her mind to the more conventional pieties of nonconformity and the placing of her sons into more secure and less killing modes of employment. Beginning well below the lowest rung of the ladder, by hardy and thrifty efforts at self-education and improvement they were launched (with the glorious and dramatic exception of Elijah Bowen whose colliery earnings kept the household going and whose unquenchable and roving sexuality saved their respectability from any sense of debt or gratitude towards him) into positions where they earned their thin bread and butter by the pen. Edwin by means of lay preaching and scholarships, hoped to attend a theological college in Wales, entering the Ministry by the skin of his teeth, Elijah's generosity and the fact of his undoubted faith. Benjamin collected insurance, scouting for the rich companies threadbare pennies from the poorest whose only possession of pounds came through the windfalls of bereavement — a not infrequent hazard. Another son was a hard working clerk in the colliery office, and the youngest, Arthur, was reaching the respected and olympian heights of schoolmastering. Aunty Sarah related their advancement to the top, second, and third rungs of the ladder with a consistency and precision of metaphor all her own.

'Well, Florrie, Edwin is still creeping — but there's a chance he'll be able to go to college in Cardiff next year. The Rev. Gwilym Jones, B.A., B.D. heard Edwin's sermon last Sunday and was most impressed, said he'd put his name forward for a scholarship.' Sarah beamed.

'What about Katie and the children?' said my grandmother caustically. There were already three children.

'Well, we'll manage, with some help from Archie. Since he's just had a rise in the office he's on carpet,' and Sarah pronounced the last word with a flourish. 'And Elijah can take over the allotments — it keeps us in fruit and vegetables — and the chickens.' It was while digging on their hillside patch of allotments that Edwin had met Katie, but neglecting the fruits of the earth for those of the flesh with such success that Aunty Sarah had arrived breathless at our house one Saturday morning to break the news of the necessary marriage in her own vein of metaphor — 'Well, with one on the way he'll have to marry this Katie, after all he's just been made a deacon, but as I said to him "You could have done better than Katie, after all, anybody can go to bed!"'

'By the way I've brought the fresh eggs. I'm afraid they're sixpence a dozen this week. The hens are broody.' Sarah smiled nervously in my grandmother's direction.

'The crusts and peelings are ready for you. I'll get them from the back pantry', was my grandmother's only reply. We carefully hoarded waste bread against Aunty Sarah's arrival. She continued with the history of her son's advancement.

'Of course Benjy's insurance round isn't very big yet. You haven't got any names for him, have you Florrie? There's not much money as he's still crawling.' I tried to picture Uncle Ben, a short, fat, red-faced gentleman, crawling around the streets on all fours collecting insurance; not appreciating my Aunt's use of metaphor I wondered why such a stance was necessary.

'How is Arthur getting on at college?' inquired my grandmother, briskly switching the conversation to the son whose academic endeavours interested her.

Aunty Sarah beamed. 'Well, he takes his Certificate this year,' she said, relishing her scholarly vocabulary. 'I think he's hoping to have a job in the Rhondda — which will be near enough to come home at the weekend,' she paused, then added joyously 'He'll be on velvet!'

The day of Aunty Sarah's visit had an additional morning excitement, for my mother made pics, often called Welsh cakes, for tea, to which Aunty Sarah stayed. It was my task to fetch the iron bakestone which we borrowed from a neighbour in the next street, and as this was rather heavy and had so small a handle that only one hand could be used in carrying it, I had often to stop for a rest on my journey, finally clambering excitedly up the steps of the backyard and into the kitchen, an exhausted Jason bearing the golden iron. By this time the fire had been well made up, and the red coals glowed: the circular slab of iron was placed over the coals, one side resting on the top of the oven and the other on the hob, built up with blackleaded fire bricks for the occasion. My mother kneaded the doughy mixture, and I assisted by adding the raisins and currants, trying not to steal too many. The cake mixture was rolled out — another stage I sometimes helped with, using an empty beer flagon we employed as rolling pin. The mixture was then cut into roughly circular shapes, and these were placed on the hot bakestone, whose surface had been sprinkled with flour. Oh the smell and savour of the baking pics, filling the kitchen as they turned to a warm, inviting brown! Picking odd corners from the hot sweet-smelling cakes, when they were almost ready, was a temptation not even burnt finger tips taught me to forego. For the cakes never seemed sweeter than at that moment when I swooped like a hungry sparrow, yet carefully lest a clumsy movement brought some loose soot down from the chimney onto the baking feast — a calamity that awaited inexpert fingers and might jolt the precariously placed iron bakestone and disturb the glowing coals. Enough cakes were baked to last several days, for my grandfather took some to work each day in his food box. For storage the cakes were carefully placed in a damp tea cloth, then deposited in our capacious stone bread pan. I found I could usually raid it each day without discovery if I took no more than three pics. Even the cat had learned, as a kitten, to enjoy the odd morsels that fell to the floor, and during the baking would sit under the armchair to one side of the fireplace, both eyes open, ready to pounce on any morsel that fell, yet safe from busy feet. On our return visits, Aunty Sarah also had a special pic-making morning, for wartime, like the earlier years of poverty, revived the necessary economies and importance of home-cooking.

Though never short of food ourselves due to my father's ex-change-and-mart in food, the long tradition of careful husbandry was kept, strictly observed by both my mother and grandmother since the lean inter-war years of strikes and low wages. 'A meal saved is as good as a meal earned,' was Florrie's curt dismissal of any of the day's meals missed, while if in a childish tantrum I refused to eat anything, 'You'll go to the food before the food will go to you,' was my grandmother's brusque but unbending reprimand. The food was returned to the pantry to await my burgeoning hunger, and what utterly and unforgettably impressed me was the literal truth of her observation. Likewise, anything left about the house, or hoarded seemingly with little or no use or purpose could be excused with the all-embracing comment 'It's all right for the time being — it won't eat nor drink'. It was a way of life where sacrifice, whether learned from chapel or hard times, was the abiding principle, especially the self-sacrifice of parents for children. This reached its apotheosis in the sacrifice entailed in their education before the post-war government introduced free Grammar School and University education as well as grants. This was a freedom heralded as a new dawn, however dubious and faltering the loyalty given in return was to prove.

But a childhood, the war, a way of life, were drawing to a close. It was a time for change, often marked as a time for dying, on the home front as well as the battlefield. Reuben was killed in a fall at the pit, Jack McCarthy carrying him out from the low seam they were working. And from this point, too, suffering for some days from shock, Jack, who was sixty-two, showed the first signs of that irreversible darkness of spirit that intimates mortality, the shadows and the shades crowding about him. Our midnight strolls down to the river became more infrequent, and Jack, always a loquacious, confident man, took to silence and brooding, his thoughts returned to the battlefields of the Somme and the Ireland of his Cork childhood. When I helped him shovel and carry the six-weekly load of coal tipped in the back lane, destined for our coal-house at the bottom of the garden, his anecdotes now were from these worlds, vivid but without laughter, true but without joy. Occasionally a miner of his generation, stopping beside the tipped heap of coal that like an obstacle of shining black stone and dust blocked the lane, would win a warm response in their chat, his heart, too, turned to the closed road back. For Jack the haunting sound of the gunfire of the battlefields still echoed.

It was June when Reuben was killed, and the sun shone warm and bright for his funeral. The neighbours crowded the length of the street, for he was a popular figure, and in the late morning the cortege set off for the hillside cemetery, several hundred men in black, fellow miners, walking in tribute and remembrance. It was the first funeral I attended, walking with my grandfather and looking across to the open window of 'The Lamb' as we reached the top of the street, seeing the full pint of beer standing alone and untouched on the sill. I pictured the kitchen friends assembled inside in suitable black, raising their half of bitter in remembrance, a ceremony where I had previously been in attendance. Last in the line of procession was Polly's husband Ianto, in his shiny black patent leather shoes. 'They'll come in handy for funerals, Ianto,' Polly had declared when he inherited them, and at the end of every funeral there was Ianto, accompanied now by a ghostly Aunty Bessie, an honoured shade still asserting women's valedictory rights.

At the graveside on that hillside of summer, the warm sunlight fired the green thoroughfares of cypress, poplar and yew bordering the centuries' tombs, cold marble embellished for resurrection. Baroque statuary for the stone dead weathered by wind and rain kept its secret as two hundred sang their hymns, in Welsh and English, at that time of paradox and parting, the dank earth of the open grave, other-worldly and melancholy song. But from bush and tree birds sang.

Afterwards most returned to the pub. Reuben's brother Ted had come all the way from Ynysybwl, and kept declaring 'I'm Ted Bell from the "bwl",' adding 'I'm not always dressed like this! See the mark where my bowler has been!' In the evening Evan the Milk, Reuben's friend, lapped up the comforts of the women's wake.

'Aunty Martha,' he lamented, 'I cried a bellyful. I cried a bellyful.'

'There you are, Evan, wipe your face with this hankie', she condoled, proffering one of Reuben's big red and white spotted handkerchiefs. 'Up there I'll be before long myself' she added, standing up for the announcement and smoothing the folds of the green plush table-cloth with the palms of her hands in the beery kitchen. She raised her glass and pointed it towards the hillside cemetery. 'I'll be joining Will Davies any day now. I can hear Will calling me.'

'Drink up girls!' said Jinny. 'Let's have another round on the old insurance!'

'With me you're staying tonight, love,' added Martha. 'You're not going back to that old house on your own.'

'Can I come, too, Aunty Martha?' pleaded Evan. 'Crying a bellyful I've been all day.'

'You can sleep in the little bedroom,' said Martha. 'But get a few flagons now to take down.'

'Are you coming down for a drink, Florrie?'

'Go and tell your mother I'll be late tonight' said my grandmother, giving me a packet of crisps.

Clutching the crisps, I raced home with the announcement.

In the early morning hours my grandmother returned, while Martha, Jinny and Evan retired in their widows' weeds to bed. Alas, they forgot to put all the lights out, and just before dawn a patrolling policeman saw the shining shoe-house at the corner of the darkened street. After some time beating on the seldom opened front door, he realised it wasn't locked and gingerly entered. Looking down on him he saw Martha and her friends standing naked at the top of the stairs: 'You must excuse us, we've been burying an old friend, Constable,' Martha announced.

But Jinny, a merry widow at sixty, turned to the future, beginning with a visit to Polly to have her fortune told. Polly told fortunes only to friends and neighbours, and by arrangement, for she would give Ianto sixpence to go to the pictures, and I usually went with him. Ianto preferred cowboy films, shouting out advice to 'Look behind you!' or 'Duck, you silly bugger!' when one of the sheriff's men behaved foolishly. His sister, Bertha, the formidable usherette who showed us to our seats, was responsible for keeping order in the cinema, brandishing her torch at the more boisterous viewers and shouting commands in a voice louder than those in the film. When things had settled down she usually came to sit by us for a chat, alerting us when an exciting moment was about to come up on the screen. She usually brought us some chocolates, for in the interval it was her job to sell them from her neatly stacked tray.

At home Polly prepared for the telling of Jinny's fortune, putting a red velvet cloth on the table, a sign her marmalade cat at once recognised, for he leapt onto the table, where he contentedly sat and purred during fortune-tellings. Polly was often consulted in these anxious times of war, and was held in some awe, her fabled second sight much respected. She could tell your fortune by reading the tea-leaves in your cup, but her preferred method was with playing cards, which she dealt gravely, her cat Bartholomew occasionally and gently putting forth an exploratory paw. Polly, it was said, had been born with a strangely veiled face, and the midwife had forecast her gifts of prediction: 'she'll see far' the remembered prophecy.

Changed into her black dress, Polly sat before the high-banked fire, staring into the coals. A pack of playing cards waited on the table. I had been present when she told family fortunes and was familiar with her metamorphosis into a woman of authority, mystery and charged voice and movement as she shuffled and then offered the cards in a wide circle to her petitioner, their signs and meanings her special wisdom.

'The dark stranger', 'the bundle', 'news across water', 'the false friend', 'the visit to a large building' were the map of my childhood dreams and I learned to dread the ace of spades.

Bartholomew opened a glittering eye. There was a nervous knock on the door.

But the ace of spades was at hand, no doubt spied by Bartholomew. Still a working miner at the coal-face, my grandfather died at sixty-three, falling downstairs during the blackout when he missed his footing on a tricky turn near the top of the stairs and the unlit landing. He lingered only a few days in the parlour, death's ante-chamber. As the funeral passed I looked for the pint at the opened window up 'The Lamb'. It stood there, but sentinel in an empty room for the sympathy was so universal that all the local men had joined the winding funeral, walking to Llan, while the kitchen friends kept my grandmother's company at home. I joined the men for a parting drink in the pub that faced the hill-top churchyard, where we had sometimes walked in summer days. By six o'clock all friends were up 'The Lamb', the two streets empty, enjoying Gugga's bequest of 'drinks all round'.

In later years I remembered that one of our paths home after

visiting the family grave was a winding lane that crossed a small
stone bridge. Here the hillside stream rushed between deep
tree-lined banks. We always sat there for a rest in summer, before
tackling a slippery muddy track, where we sometimes clambered
along the hedgerows to find the memorial stone simply marked
'Cadair Edward II'. This 'chair of Edward II', a rough hewn stone
somewhere between a milestone and a headstone was often
hidden deep in the grassy bank and difficult to find in green and
leafy summer months. Local legend had it that Edward II, fleeing
the victorious barons en route for Ireland, hid up the tree as they
passed on the track below. A likely story I later learned, studying
Marlowe's *Edward II* at school, for spied by a Welsh valley mower,
Marlowe relates, he was betrayed and discovered while seeking
refuge in Neath Abbey, some miles westward. Unknown to us
both it was a stroll of rare pilgrimage to a unique memorial!

It was a few days after my grandfather's funeral that my father,
who had always feared Jack McCarthy, announced '*I'm* going to
perform now!' 'Are you?' declared my grandmother rising from
her armchair by the fire, and always more than a match for him.
'Then you can perform in the street!' He soon left, and we all
settled down to a quieter, non-violent life, albeit poorer. We now
had to watch the pennies for the first time, my grandmother on
her widow's pension, and though a successful business man due
to his exchange and mart in meat, farm produce and whisky, my
father gave only niggardly support to my mother, sister and me.
Fortunately there were free school dinners, and in later years I
gained a University State Scholarship, my father refusing to
support me, to counter the market spirit.

By now there were almost daily triumphs in the war, and each
day under my grandmother's direction and to our growing
elation, our circle of flags on the kitchen wall grew tighter, the
many-coloured circumference narrowing to the centre of Berlin.
We knew there would soon be rejoicing and parties. There was a
new excitement in the air; we were preparing bunting for a victory
display in the street. I had kept a diary during the war years, and
latterly it noted only victories. My entry for Friday, 5 January
1945 reads: 'Had a fight. Fighting in Athens stops'. Tuesday, 16:
'Russians 50 miles from German border'. Wednesday, 17:

'Russians capture Warsaw. Went to pantomime in Cardiff', Wednesday, 24: 'British 20 miles from Mandalay. Heaviest snowfall last night for years. 1½ feet deep in street.' I see that on the 29th we were '13 miles from Mandalay', and on 1st February 'Russians 40 miles from Berlin. I had my dungarees'. Daily the war news is faithfully recorded: 23 March, 'British cross Rhine. I now practise piano ½ hour every night'. March 29: 'Russians reach Austrian frontier. Frankfurt ours.' Friday, 27 April: 'Russians and Americans meet, Italian Patriots capture Milan, Turin, Genoa.' 28 April: 'Himmler offers surrender to all Powers except Russia but they say no.' On Tuesday, 8 May, the diary records 'The German war is ended. Germans sign unconditional surrender. Granny went up the pub early. I went with her. We stayed there all day.' It was my last entry. Up the market, my father had a celebratory auction of meat, sausages, and tripe. 'It's the last day!' hailed Morgan joyously, 'Everything must go!'

From our house hung a giant Union Jack that had once graced the local town hall, and alongside it a home-made Russian flag, a sheet dyed red with a roughly cut sickle in yellow material sewn on. The memory of this provoked from Labour Party canvassers, during the election campaign that followed the win in Europe, the remark, 'Don't bother to knock there boys — they're all Communists!' After the street parties and Victory celebrations the red flag became a cushion cover that I appropriated for my parlour study.

Soon there was a new government, and when the election results were announced my grandmother declared a spectacular party: two barrels of beer in the cwtch after she led friends and family from 'The Lamb', even respectable neighbours openly watching our progress down the street. Once everybody had a glass of beer Florrie took the centre of the room and recited from 'Locksley Hall', her ringing tones celebrating the idealism born of sacrifice and war:

> For I dipt into the future, far as human eye could see,
> Saw the Vision of the world, and all the wonder that would
> be;
> Saw the heavens fill with commerce, argosies of magic sails,
> Pilots of the purple twilight, dropping down with costly bales...

With the standards of the people plunging thro' the
    thunder storm...
Till the war-drum throbb'd no longer, and the battleflags
    were furl'd
In the Parliament of man, the Federation of the world.

Strangely absent from the party, as from 'The Lamb' of late, was
Evan the Milk. Suddenly he had stopped coming, for no reason
I knew, disappearing into what death, adventures or nameless
streets of his despair — perhaps into the mothering milk — he
alone could tell. But I missed Dando, his loyal old horse who drew
the milk cart and whose company I kept in the pub yard to the
end of long, hazy afternoons.

My grandmother insisted on travelling to London for the State
Opening of Parliament. We waited patiently, and with as much a
sense of victory and triumph, hope too, as the ending of the war
in Europe had given us, there on the pavement in Downing Street.
With quiet pride and barely controlled excitement we watched
the new Labour administration leave Number 10 for the House
of Commons. On my grandmother's face showed a deeper sense
of fulfilment and joy than I had known before as she pointed to
the passing government cars, indicating to me the presence of
such celebrities as Clement Attlee, Sir Stafford Cripps, Ellen
Wilkinson, and the loved folk hero of the mining valleys, the
silver-tongued Nye Bevan.

For Florrie was it a dawn that would belie the false dawns, an
end of the days of the turncoat, the mean-spirited, the exploiter;
for did not the years and times she'd known of bitter experience
sow fruitful seeds too? Clutching her hand, I thought of the
promise of that other recent revelation on the night when the end
of the blackout was announced. Then I wondered, with mounting
excitement at the illumination of the street lamps, was it only
childhood that had gone out into the darkness when the lights
finally came on that evening with a hint of sorcery. Looking down
at the lost, day-dreaming eleven-year-old proudly beside her on
the pavement as the crowds began to disperse my grandmother
smiled, then sternly declared: 'Mind you, the world is round',
words I only heard on that momentous day but becoming clearer
with the years. And the paths through the tall trees and tales to

the childwood ghosts, like the sounds of that first river haunt still, keeping the gift of love.

And in the shared dark I delight to imagine them up 'The Lamb'.

Acknowledgements

An extract 'Friends and Neighbours' appeared in *King's College Review* in 1955. 'The Golden Hatchets' was published in *Critical Quarterly* in 1987, and 'The Kitchen Friends' in *New Welsh Review* in 1996.

I am grateful to the Industrial and Martime Museum, Cardiff for the supply of and permission to reprint the photograph of Garth Colliery.